# WORKING WORLD 101

# THE NEW GRAD'S GUIDE TO GETTING A JOB

Bridget Graham and Monique Reidy

adamsmedia
avon, massachusetts

Published by
Adams Media, a division of F+W Media, Inc.
57 Littlefield Street, Avon, MA 02322. U.S.A.
*www.adamsmedia.com*

ISBN 10: 1-59869-495-2
ISBN 13: 978-1-59869-495-6

Printed in the United States of America.

J I H G F E D C B A

**Library of Congress Cataloging-in-Publication Data**
is available from the publisher.

This publication is designed to provide accurate and authoritative information with regard to the subject matter covered. It is sold with the understanding that the publisher is not engaged in rendering legal, accounting, or other professional advice. If legal advice or other expert assistance is required, the services of a competent professional person should be sought.
—From a *Declaration of Principles* jointly adopted
by a Committee of the American Bar Association
and a Committee of Publishers and Associations

Many of the designations used by manufacturers and sellers to distinguish their product are claimed as trademarks. Where those designations appear in this book and Adams Media was aware of a trademark claim, the designations have been printed with initial capital letters.

Lyrics on page 23 are from the song "Etcetera Whatever,"
by Over the Rhine. Copyright © 1996 by Over the Rhine/Scampering
Songs Publishing. ASCAP. Used by permission.

*This book is available at quantity discounts for bulk purchases.*
*For information, please call 1-800-289-0963.*

# CONTENTS

# Acknowledgments

I'D LIKE TO THANK MONIQUE for taking this adventure with me. We've come a long way from sitting in the coffee shop saying, "We should write a book for college graduates!" I thank my parents for always encouraging and supporting me no matter what path I choose to pursue; your love and encouragement mean the world to me. I thank my friends for their support, especially Lisa, who has been very good to me. I have so many wonderful people in my life who are excited for me when I achieve, and it means the world: Marie, Muge, Maria, Helen, Mr. and Mrs. A, and Scinde (I miss our walks), Kjersti and Marc (and Toby and Leo, whom I am honored to love, are a given, of course); your joy in my projects is always so encouraging. (A special thanks to Jake.) Thanks to Laura who let me take the journey of writing I always wanted to take. I thank Can for the help he gave me while I was reaching for my goals. Thanks to our book agent, Uwe Stender at TriadaUS, who believed in our project. I also want to thank Brittney and Traci for offering me a dream job even though it came along at an inopportune time (that I didn't initially see coming); I can't tell you how much I would have loved it. I thank all the HR friends and store managers along the way in my career who helped me grow to the next level. I have the knowledge to write this because of you. To Maria K. who long ago on a rooftop told me to "seize my place at the table"; I have never forgotten this piece of advice. And I thank God for letting my dreams come true. Here's to happy jobs and happy careers!

—*Bridget*

MANY OF US HAVE FACED a particularly overwhelming subject matter in life that has elicited an "I could write a book!" statement. In my case, I've watched as my three twentysomething daughters struggled with the challenges that confront young job seekers and have learned that landing a rewarding career is not an event that automatically happens even if you hold a college degree. I am grateful to Tawny, Nicole, and Kimmy for their resolve to follow their professional dreams even though it involves a multitude of trials and frustrations, and for their help and inspiration with this book project. I am also thankful to Steve, my supportive husband who has been a source of help and reassurance, and who has had to fend for himself on numerous occasions throughout this past year while I was busy writing. I'm so fortunate to have friends who were genuinely interested in the progression of this assignment and who have encouraged me at every turn. I especially appreciate Patty, Rita, Dave, and Judith, who have been a tremendous support system. And had it not been for my aunt Nelly, who on numerous occasions drove across town to feed my three dogs, I probably would not have had the luxury of working uninterrupted, as I was able to do. I am also thankful to Bridget, whose expertise in HR has been invaluable and whose sense of humor helped make the hours we spent working together so much more enjoyable. And finally, a big thanks to Uwe Stender, who constantly propelled us forward and worked tirelessly with us to see this book come to fruition.

—*Monique*

WE BOTH WANT TO EXTEND a very special thank you to the corporate and young professionals who have agreed to be interviewed and have allowed us to share their experiences in this book.

# Introduction

You're graduating from college and it's a wonderfully exciting time for you; the college years are coming to an end, and there is a career filled with possibilities ahead of you. You are a well-prepared, knowledgeable generation, and there are many reasons for you to be proud. You have so much to give and we want to make sure your expectations are met when you search for your first job!

This book came about when both of us returned to graduate school after many years in the working world. We heard your questions on how to begin a job search as we sat with your peers in class, and we discovered ideas and tips that *Working World 101* will pass along to you.

You may not even have thought to ask some of the questions we'll be answering, but we know what interviewers will be asking and the qualifications they want. Bridget Graham has spent more than thirteen years working in human resources, and Monique Reidy has worked as an advertising director and owned and managed a design firm with clients such as the L.A. Dodgers, the USC football team, Showtime Networks, Amgen, and others. Between the two of us, we've hired countless managers and terminated those who "just didn't get it." Our expertise will help you navigate through the job search, interview, and beyond, and we will also share real-world advice about what companies—big and small—are looking for when hiring.

With all our experience, we understand that your generation is unique. We know you are confident, optimistic, civic minded, and techno savvy. Your generation respects competent individuals, not titled ones. Here's the thing: the people hiring you are Gen X and Baby Boomers, and there are some adjustments that will have to be made. Knowing that generational differences exist is of tremendous value as you begin your job search.

Even when talking with professionals about this book, we found generational differences. Baby Boomers have one set of preferences for what they want to see; Gen X individuals have another. No one is right and no one is wrong, but understanding this helps. Ask employers (or hiring managers), and *most* will tell you they know they need to tailor their companies and styles for your generation. Most know that within six months of working you've already decided if a company is right for you. Most know that your goal is to find a job and a life with meaning, not to work for the same company for twenty-five years—and this is okay. But employers expect professionalism. They want to know, even if you're only planning on working for two years before heading on to the next company or even off to backpack in Africa, that during the time at their company you're giving 110 percent and contributing to the growth of projects, clients, and the company.

You thrive on change and movement; you want rapid career growth and experiences to help take you to the next step, and then the step after that. Companies are beginning to understand and want to provide this for you. Because of this, a little research is worthwhile to make sure you not only find the right career but also the right company. This is where networking, informational interviews, continuous research and, of course, professional communication come into play.

This is a book about getting your first job, but unlike other books for recent grads, we focus on the importance of communication during the job search and within the workplace. Before you even snag an interview, your resume will help you sell yourself to a prospective boss. The way you dress, how you speak, your nonverbal cues—all of these communicate who you are.

So don't just think of this as a "how-to" job search guide. This book will be a doorway into evaluating your communication style, too! Resumes full of grammatical errors won't even get you an initial call. Miscellaneous speech blunders and qualifiers such as "like" and "do you know what I mean" and ending every sentence as a question diminish your credibility. (Think about this last one . . . you may not even realize you do this. When you say an affirmative statement, see if your voice inflection trails up. Does it sounds as though you're asking a question, even though you're stating a fact?)

Communication is key, and with this book you'll learn the art of verbal finesse—an art that will take you from the dorm room to the boardroom in record time. You'll learn how to communicate to others that you are strong, confident, capable, and ready to take this next step in your life's journey. You want to be an agent of change and find the fulfilling career you're seeking. We know you're fed up with a lot of what you hear about corporate scandals, politics, and behaviors, but in order to be the difference-maker you long to be (and also to make the salary you want), you have to first show the employer you have what it takes and get your foot in the door.

You've already earned the college degree, and now we want to help you get on the right path with your communication toolbox properly packed. You want to be vocal but also realistic. With this book, you'll find practical resume and interview advice. There are inspirational stories, gender-specific pitfalls and successes, and more. From making contact to dressing the part to saying the right thing, here are the scripts and tips to help you on your way to career success!

PART ONE

# Would I Hire Me?

# CHAPTER 1

# A Degree of Daring

## CONFIDENCE IS KEY

"What's the worst thing that can happen to a quarterback? He loses his confidence."

TERRY
BRADSHAW

Having just finished college, you've probably learned to typecast people based on their personality traits. You may have also learned to appreciate those classmates who achieved success in their chosen fields of study. Or you may have developed real friendships with people who encouraged others and seemed to always be in a good mood. Maybe you wish you could be like them.

These young men and women most likely have a strong self-image and a healthy dose of confidence. As handy as these qualities were during your academic years, now that you're job hunting, these traits will become even more valuable. While you don't want to present yourself as arrogant, even more detrimental to your success is the common and debilitating quality of self-doubt.

## BE CERTAIN OF YOUR ABILITY

When a reference about confidence is made, it usually refers to self-confidence—a certainty about your ability to succeed. This essential quality is closely linked to one equally valuable: self-esteem. It's a challenge to have a solid sense of self-confidence if you do not have a strong sense of your own identity and value.

You've likely heard the maxim: hurt (adjective) people hurt (verb) people. By the same token, confident people build others up to be confident. Maybe this is why the most self-assured kids in school were usually the most popular. Like magnets they attracted equally bubbly people. When it comes to job hunting, the more enthusiastic you come across to a prospective employer, the more likely you are to stand out from the other applicants. All other issues being equal, self-confidence is usually what sets a successful person apart from someone less successful.

Rick Pitino, the former Kentucky Wildcats coach who led his team to the 1996 national basketball championship, once noted: " . . . you can expect great things from people who feel good about themselves. They can push themselves. They can set long-term goals. They have dreams everyone expects to be fulfilled. People with high self-esteem are risk-takers, but more important, they are achievers." And you can bet most employers agree with him.

In order to present yourself as self-assured in a job interview, you'll need to assess your self-confidence. This highly charismatic quality shows through in a variety of ways, from your body language to your tone of voice, your ability to make and hold eye contact, what you say, and how you say it.

People who are not self-confident are easy to spot. They generally depend excessively on the approval of others in order to feel good about themselves. They fear defeat and rejection and often avoid taking risks because they are afraid to fail. But what's most noticeable is that they generally do not expect to be successful.

Amy, a graduate of a notable university in the Southeast, confesses to feeling academically competent but lacking the confidence to face the challenges of the real world. "I graduated summa cum laude and was sure of my ability to make good grades and turn in assignments that were above average," she explains. "But when I started to look for work, I realized I wasn't so competent in nonacademic areas, and I felt overwhelmed and just withdrew." Like Amy, many of you may feel like a fish out of water upon graduation. You may have felt cocooned in the comfort of peers and a familiar collegiate environment, but once out, you may have lost your footing. It can only take a couple of negative experiences to send a recent grad down the dangerous spiral of self-doubt.

## SAY NO TO SELF-DOUBT

Self-doubt is the antithesis of self-confidence. Other bad habits, such as constantly putting yourself down, develop from this destructive habit. If you're prone to this, you need to make a deliberate effort to quiet those negative thoughts by catching yourself and rephrasing what you say in your head. For example, if you have a tendency to discount yourself, you may talk yourself out of applying for a particular position with thoughts like: "Why should I bother sending my resume? I'll just be rejected again anyhow" or "I'll skip this opportunity because that company is probably seeking someone more capable than I am." If you tend to be negative, ask a good friend to pay attention to your conversations and bring pessimistic statements to your attention. When you catch yourself in the act of talking and thinking pessimistically, you can willfully work on becoming more positive and dynamic.

Self-doubt, negative talk, and a focus on failure all nurture a poor self-image. People who lack self-esteem still have the same desires as those who are confident, but they often remain dissatisfied because they are afraid to take risks and establish goals. A lack of self-confidence does not necessarily translate to lack of ability, though. Often it is an excessive focus on others and their accomplishments that makes you feel you can never measure up. Maybe your parents set standards too high and you could never quite please them. Perhaps you've had professors who were condescending and you learned to withdraw for fear of further criticism. The good news is that no matter where your lack of confidence comes from you can restore your self-image and level of self-sufficiency!

No one is born confident. Confidence requires a considerable amount of affirmation from your family and other significant people in your life in order to develop. If you have low self-esteem, it's liberating to know that people aren't thinking about you nearly as often as they're thinking about themselves. As you go about your day, substitute the internal question "What will people think of me if I do this?" with an affirming statement such as "People are more concerned about how they appear to others and are not focused on me and what I do."

Keep in mind that your past won't change, but your future can, if you have the right mindset and properly manage your destiny. Your sense of self-assurance is affected not only by what has happened to you but by how you interpret those events. Since this has a direct bearing on your level of self-esteem, you can learn to change your perspective about your past and decide to overcome those setbacks.

Remember, having a *realistic* assessment of who you are, what you can truly offer, and the wonderful qualities you possess will help propel you to a successful career.

## CLASS NOTES

Arica, 24

Knowing which specific industry she wanted to work in, Arica graduated from a trade-specific school, the Fashion Institute. She worked
in a retail position while earning her degree, which not only provided her valuable knowledge but also **networking opportunities**.
Her current job, a sales and marketing specialist for a top denim
company, was attained via a contact from a previous position. "Job
boards didn't work for me," she says. "Sometimes to get the right
job, it is about coming across as confident and keeping contacts with
those who know people within the industry."

Arica took advantage of every opportunity. While working in a retail
store, an owner of a prominent clothing line came into the locale and
she "got the guts up" to go talk to him and share that she was pursuing a corporate-level retail job. He gave her his card and the name of
a person to contact at the company. Within a few days, she had an
interview and was offered the position. She wasn't able to take the
position because she was still finishing classes, but she knew that
she'd be able to use the **confidence the interview gave her** when
she was actually looking for a job.

"It's about **stepping out of your comfort zone** and asking people:
'If you're looking to hire someone, I'd love to send you my resume,'"
she says.

## WRITE DOWN YOUR SUCCESSES

Here's an exercise to help beef up your self-esteem and/or keep it in perspective: Get a notebook or create a spreadsheet document on your computer. Call the notebook or document "My Success Story." Within those blank pages, label one "Victories." On this page, outline every imaginable achievement you have ever enjoyed. Did you ace a difficult class? Have you traveled to places you had wished to visit? Did you run a 10k? Begin your list by noting that you've completed college and have earned your degree—a feat many people cannot claim!

Continue to add to this list as new triumphs come to mind. Whether grand or small, each event you are proud of should be noted. Refer to this list often and you'll be amazed at how quickly you develop a winning attitude. Celebrate and take pleasure in your successes, and formulate strong mental pictures about yourself, your past achievements, and your goals. Frequently reading through your list will help you focus on your positive points as you learn to reconsider your negatives.

### ADVICE FROM THE CORNER OFFICE
Susan Sellani-Hosage, a senior manager in human resources, suggests, "Don't speak in 'we' terminology. If I were hiring you and your whole team back at the office, that would be great, but I'm not. Defining your individual contributions in your previous job is critical in creating the impression that will get you your next one."

Label your next page or section "Power Points." Here, list any desirable attributes you possess. Do you have a good sense of humor? Are you artistic? Are you a genius with electronics? Jot down as many positive things about yourself that come to mind. Consider compliments you have received or talents easily attainable to you. Are you a math whiz? A gourmet cook? If it's a strong point write it down.

When you show up for a job interview you should have your achievements clearly in mind. Don't negate your achievements by not remembering what they are. Your lists of "Victories" and "Power Points" will help prepare you for any questions that come your way as you'll be ready to fire off your most notable qualities and accomplishments with ease.

**KNOW YOUR OBSTACLES**

Label another page "Obstacles." Here list any events in your life that may have been barriers to success. Did you fail a class? Did you not make the basketball team? Were you denied admission to the college of your dreams? Any event, great or small, that you consider to be an impediment to your success should be noted on this page.

Your "Obstacles" list is *not* one you'll want to revisit often, but you should utilize it to help you rise above your unfortunate circumstances and change your point of view. Take each event and note why you believe you came to that regrettable outcome. Were your goals too unrealistic? Did you score low on your SATs because you did not prepare properly? Were you fired from a previous job because you were repeatedly late?

Once you have outlined your unlucky occurrences, noting the likely reasons for the adverse outcome, have a conversation with yourself about why things turned out the way they did. For example, "I scored low on my SATs because I did not take the time required to prepare, and that's why the application to my favorite university was declined. I was not denied admission because I am an idiot but because I did not plan accordingly. Next time I have an important exam I will make the required effort."

This rationale will help you realize that you have a great deal of potential and—given the proper tools—the ability to succeed. Balancing this exercise with reaffirming your achievements will help you form a healthy self-view and you will become more confident as a result. If you have suffered extraordinary trauma or have experienced events you believe you cannot overcome on your own, consider visiting a counselor who can help you make sense of those experiences.

You may be asking what this has to do with job hunting. The answer is a great deal! Until you learn to overcome your past and decide to have a confident and positive attitude, the less likely you are to land the position you want.

Before you put away your notebook, label a final page "Moving Ahead." Here list your goals and the dreams you hope to realize. Confident people are always stretching forward, seeking to improve and grow. Noting what you want to work toward will give you purpose and self-assurance.

Mastering the notion of confidence is a valuable lesson because these skills can help you in every endeavor in life, not just with your job search. Confidence doesn't come naturally for some people; most lean toward the modest side, being careful not to come across as smug. Others appear too confident, without having anything to back it up. This is only perceived as arrogance, and will cause another set of problems. This is why you want to appreciate *exactly* who you are and what accomplishments you have achieved.

Once you've learned to appreciate your own sense of achievement, you'll exude a noticeable poise others will surely pick up on. Believe in yourself and be proud of your experiences because they have helped to mold you into who you are today! And when you walk into an interview with a healthy self-assurance, you'll surely chalk up points in your favor.

There's nothing more frustrating to an interviewer than having to work hard to get an interviewee to open up and share about him or herself. It can be exasperating, and the one characteristic you don't want someone to attribute to you is exasperation! You want to leave each meeting knowing you've sent a powerful message about your level of self-confidence and your ability to handle the position for which you're applying.

Think of self-esteem as a muscle you have to develop for the rest of your life. Like a muscle, the more you use your confidence, the stronger it becomes. As you continue to accomplish great feats in your personal and professional life, you will feel better about yourself and your confidence will increase. Work at it and strive for it and your level of confidence will strengthen and escalate. ■

## cheat sheet

Don't come off as arrogant.

Don't fear defeat.

Do take risks.

Do have confidence in your abilities and skills.

Do paint a realistic picture of your accomplishments.

Don't be self-condescending.

Don't engage in negative self-talk.

## CHAPTER 2

# Your Real-Life Transcript

## SELF-ASSESSMENT MAKES SENSE

You've got the college degree, fashionable interview attire, and a flashy new briefcase. Now it's time to get started. First, it's time to stop and take a personal and professional inventory. This is important because you should be aware of all you have to offer to an employer. Taking stock of your experiences, situations, and achievements will help propel you to success. But first you need to assess other necessary qualities: What are your talents, gifts, strengths, and passions? What do you consider your weaknesses? Are there tasks that don't appeal to you? Listing these qualities will help you solidify what you're looking for in a job.

### DO YOU KNOW YOURSELF?

First, determine your value system. Are you honest? Loyal? Do you possess integrity? The following is a quick quiz designed to help you determine your strengths and weaknesses for an enlightening evaluation.

1. A bag of money falls off a truck in front of you. You . . .
   a. Leave immediately and book a flight to Barbados.
   b. Sneak it home, hold it for a few days, and eventually turn back in some of it (after buying your mom a car).
   c. Flag down the truck and give it back.
2. If you broke something at a store, you would . . .
   a. Try to put it back together.
   b. Blame it on the person you're with.
   c. Fess up to the crime.
3. If you missed the due date for a term paper, did you . . .
   a. Quickly withdraw from the class.
   b. Make up a story about your computer having multiviruses.
   c. Tell the professor the truth and take accountability for being late.

Okay, this obviously isn't a scientific evaluation, but it does make you assess your values and personal characteristics. If you answered mostly C, you're likely an honest candidate (congratulations!). If you answered mostly A or B, you should probably re-evaluate your priorities and principles.

**A Closer Look**
Let's be sure we're all on the same page regarding the definitions of these terms:

*Accountability:* The ability to fess up when you need to—you're able to say you did it (or didn't do it).

*Ethics:* Ask yourself . . . if you read about your actions on the front page of the *New York Times*, will you appear ethical? Did you/do you take the high road?

*Honesty:* You tell the truth even if you take a little heat.

*Integrity:* Having the knowledge and wherewithal to do all of the above.

It's easy to say, "Of course, I'm honest!" But when it comes time to show your personal character, those insecurities and fears pop through! This is when you take a deep breath and check your insecurities at the door . . . for good. Determine who you are, believe in yourself, and stick to your guns (and values!).

In an interview, you're probably not going to have tremendous opportunities to display your honesty, integrity, and ethical superqualities, but you don't want to walk into an interview without having confidence in them. You want to be confident in the knowledge that you are a true asset to the company.

PERSONAL INVENTORY CHECKLIST
- ❒ I am honest.
- ❒ I am ethical.
- ❒ I present myself in a professional manner.
- ❒ I am well groomed.
- ❒ I check my insecurities at the door.

## DO YOU HAVE AN ATTITUDE?

A little bit of attitude goes a long way, and it's much better to have the positive kind. It's cliché, but smile through the phone when speaking to a prospective employer; it really will put a positive lift in your voice. Another trick (it works on first dates, too): Before walking into an interview, visualize three people who think the world of you. Then enter confidently and let the person you're about to meet "see" those qualities, too. Always remember that knowing and understanding who you are is just as important as how many words you can type and which computer programs you know.

## WHAT IS YOUR FIRST IMPRESSION?

The first impression you make is everything, and if you make a bad one, it is often impossible to recover. Use the power of the first impression to your advantage. You want to create a winning image with your physical presentation in addition to your job skills. You may be the most qualified person for the position, but if an employer is offended by your breath or can smell your body odor from down the hall, it will work against you.

A potential employer should consider you a complete package. Your skills and experience, your ability to listen and make eye contact, your posture and physical presentation all work together to tell who you are as an applicant. Remember, you are the product, and during the interview your goal is to sell yourself to those who have the authority to hire you. Like it or not, your overall appearance has an impact on your interviewer's opinion, especially in those first crucial thirty seconds of an introduction. Not everyone is a beauty queen or an Adonis, but in this case it's less about beauty and more about how well put together you are.

## WHAT'S YOUR APPEARANCE?

Be sure to take inventory of your closet, too. A professional wardrobe is a must, but this doesn't mean a stuffy, conservative wardrobe. If you take a position in a design or advertising firm versus an accounting firm, the dress code may be more relaxed, but it still needs to be professional.

There will be more on clothing in Chapter 8, but for now take just a simple inventory. Do you have a professional wardrobe? Take all your clothes out of your closet and lay them on your bed. Set aside anything that looks more appropriate for Saturday night than Monday morning.

What's left? Do the remaining pieces mix and match? You don't need to go out and buy a new whole wardrobe, but at this point you need to look at what you do have. Make sure you have a few outfits appropriate for the interview. And you'll want to have some professional pieces ready in case you get the job and you have to hit the office before you have a chance to hit the mall.

*Women:* Do you have at least three to five skirts that can be worn with at least three to five tops? Do you have at least three to five pants able to be worn with a variety of tops? You don't need to have a multitude of clothes to have a full wardrobe. The key is to have items able to create numerous outfits, but have a few wild cards in there, too. Have some fun items to dress up a work outfit, keeping the overall look practical.

*Men:* Are you looking for a job requiring a suit each day, or do you prefer a position where you can dress more casual? Either way, do you have basic button-down shirts to wear with different pants (or suits)? Are ties required on the job? Do you have ties with color for a little fun? Do those ties match a variety of shirts? Are you taking a position where you can wear colored shirts, or should all your shirts be white?

Take inventory of your closet in regards to what position you want. Make sure your wardrobe matches the job, as well as the other clothing pieces next to it.

### Ah, the Smell of It

In addition to how you look, pay attention to how you smell. As insensitive as it may sound, people who have an offensive scent don't always know it. It seems simple, but make sure you take a shower, put on deodorant, and brush your teeth before you head out to your interview. To be on the safe side, you may want to chew on a breath mint right before you walk in. (This is basic, but you'd be surprised how many "educated" people just don't understand this!)

### Let Me Take Your Hand

Nails are an often overlooked detail for the interviewee. Dirt under the fingernails and the phone number you have inked on your hand from Saturday night just won't fly. You'll be shaking hands with your interviewer so a grimy palm will count against you. A firm handshake will not go unnoticed if someone feels the need to sanitize after shaking a perspiring palm. If you have chronically sweaty palms, consult with your physician about the remedies available to treat your condition.

### Other Appearances

You want the interviewer to focus on your qualifications and competence, not distractions like chewing gum, excessive jewelry, or overpowering cologne or perfume. If you have prominent tattoos or body piercings, cover these up prior to your interview.

Remember, before you walk into your prospective place of business for an interview take a hard, realistic look at yourself. Your outfit will send an unspoken message about who you are, and your personal cleanliness conveys your attention to detail. You'll feel confident in yourself if you've taken the necessary inventory and know what you have to offer.

## YOUR PROFESSIONAL INVENTORY

Okay, now you're feeling and looking good, so it's time to evaluate what other skills are necessary to be successful in the workplace. Taking a professional inventory includes evaluating your work ethic and what you bring to the workplace. Remember, it's always a good idea to develop solid habits from the get-go so you can take these valuable features with you throughout your professional life.

> PROFESSIONAL INVENTORY CHECKLIST
> ❐ I am willing to learn.
> ❐ I am able to take direction from authority/managers.
> ❐ I know the relevant skills of the field I'm working in.
> ❐ I am organized.
> ❐ I am able to communicate.
> ❐ I give 110 percent no matter the task at hand.

Are you a clock-watcher, or are you committed to finishing a job even if it takes you beyond your 5:00 P.M. day? Staying on top of your projects, finishing what you start, and delivering what is expected of you are valuable characteristics of a hard-working employee, and your boss will notice whether or not you fit this bill.

It can be difficult to take orders from others. What is your threshold for listening to authority? Do you have problems being told what to do? Here's a handy hint: If you're working for somebody, you're going to have to learn to follow instructions. You can't think taking directions is beneath you. You are being paid to do what you are asked, so it's important to listen up and do the best job you can. Plus, when it comes time for promotion, the best person gets the job. Are you able to work like you're already in the job you want?

"Kristen" understood this concept. She didn't like her current department or her current entry-level position. She wanted to be transferred into another, highly competitive, area for her dream job. When a position opened, she was tapped for it. Why? Because she saw the bigger picture and was one of the best in a position she didn't even want to be in. She would have never been promoted if she were lazy, unenthusiastic, or unproductive while waiting for the "right" job.

While evaluating your work ethic, you should also determine what your habits are when no one's watching. Do you surf the net? Can others feel comfortable leaving their belongings in your possession without worrying you might take a peek? Do you try to justify making personal long-distance phone calls on the company line? A good habit to develop early on is to imagine someone is *always* watching you. This notion will keep you honest if you tend to have entitlement issues.

Are you organized? This is a very subjective term, and what may be messy to one person is a pile of common sense to another. However, as a competent employee, it's important to have a clutter-free space and the organization required to conduct your job effectively and efficiently. Misplacing business cards, losing important notes, and forgetting deadlines are simply not acceptable.

Are you punctual? Some people seem to always run a few minutes late, no matter what, but this won't fly in the workplace. Revise your internal definition of punctuality to mean the following: not a second past the time you are expected to show up at a meeting or finish a project.

Can you communicate? When asked a question, you should respond clearly, concisely, and with confidence. Later chapters will help clarify and define good communication, but know that this is an extremely important skill to have in order to be taken seriously—by both peers and supervisors—in the work environment.

Have you figured out the proper logistics? Do you have a professional e-mail address and private voicemail line? Create a new e-mail if necessary, but anything sexually suggestive, of a party nature, or even of a lazy nature (one address on a resume was josephsleeps@ . . .) is not appropriate.

When you take your professional and personal inventory, ask yourself: Who are you and what do you stand for? What image are you communicating to employers and coworkers? Know what is in your inventory toolbox so you can put your best face forward. ■

## cheat sheet

Do make a great first impression!

Don't work poorly in one position thinking "if only I was in another."

Do be sure of who you are and what you have to offer to an employer.

Do determine your value system and who you are when no one else is around.

Don't try to tell about all your great qualifications without first doing inventory of what these may be.

CHAPTER 3

# The Employment Expedition

## JUMP-START YOUR JOB SEARCH

> "And courage
> is a weapon
> we must use
> to find some
> life you can't
> refuse."
>
> —OVER THE
> RHINE
>
> From the song
> "Etcetera
> Whatever"

Starting your job search may seem like a daunting task, so create timelines and realistic goals. Start with a daily goal, rather than a weekly goal, so it is attainable. Every day, make a pact with yourself to send out two resumes or make two calls. (Of course, you can choose a higher number; just make sure it is realistic for you and your current schedule.) There are many outlets available to help you in your search for a job; utilize them all!

### NETWORKING (NOT THE TV KIND)

Did you know about 40 percent of new hires come from employee referrals? Most available jobs are never advertised, so it's not always what you know but whom you know that will help you land your dream job. This doesn't mean that you should avoid hard work, making phone calls, and following up in your job search. But networking is one of the most important activities you'll spend your time doing.

Don't let the word "networking" freak you out. It's nothing more than doing what you did so much of in college: talking to people, exploring ideas, and making contacts. However, instead of doing this to advance your social or academic goals, you'll now network to promote your professional ambitions.

Plainly defined, networking is just genuinely being interested in people and talking with them. From this, you can find an opportunity to listen for an opportunity to pitch what you have to offer (in this case yourself, your talents, your education, and your experience), but only after you've established some real human connection. Before you get too nervous, here's what networking isn't:

- It is NOT begging for a job.
- It is NOT a task confined only to a giant ballroom filled with executives.
- It is NOT an activity reserved just for extroverted people.
- It is NOT a random, thoughtless process.
- It is NOT contacting people you don't know asking for a job.

A typical conversation in which connections are made may be as straightforward as the following:

MRS. RAY: Hello, Kyle! I haven't seen you in ages. How's your mom?

KYLE: She's well. She's actually thrilled now that I've finished college!

MRS. RAY: Oh, that's great, congratulations!

KYLE: Thank you. Now I'm in the process of finding work in marketing.

MRS. RAY: Is this what your degree is in?

KYLE: Yes, and I'm hoping to land a position with a major corporation here in town. Do you know anyone in the marketing field?

MRS. RAY: I don't know anyone in marketing. But my neighbor is the CEO of a biotech firm, and I could ask her.

KYLE: I'd be happy to send you a copy of my resume if you wouldn't mind passing it along to her.

MRS. RAY: Of course! I think your mom might have my address, but if not, let me give it to you . . .

Basically, you network when you tell everyone you know that you're looking for a job and, more specifically, the type of work you're hoping to find. Family, friends, former professors, and neighbors may know someone who knows someone, and people love to help those who come across as sincere and motivated.

**ADVICE FROM THE CORNER OFFICE**
**La'Trise Smith, assistant vice president of human resources at Huntington Bank, reminds:**

- **Networking is not an unpleasant chore: It isn't a task or an obligation.**
- **Seize every opportunity to talk to people: It isn't just about talking at an event; you can be at the bus stop or in line at a bank.**
- **Utilize every opportunity when talking to someone to let them know who you are.**

Once you are comfortable speaking with those you know, move on to those you don't—whomever you find yourself talking with during a typical day. Instead of asking someone for a job, ask for advice and listen intently. Most people love talking about themselves, so use this opportunity to ask questions about their professional choices and how they attained those positions.

Once you get it down, networking shouldn't take a lot of extra time out of your life and should easily fit into your natural communication during your ordinary day. The most casual connections are often the most rewarding, and those generally happen numerous times throughout a typical week.

**ADVICE FROM THE CORNER OFFICE**
**Susan Sellani-Hosage, a senior manager in human resources, uses this exercise to help job seekers think about their image: "I ask students to raise their hands if they have friends. (All of them naturally do.) I ask them to keep their hands raised if they would recommend all of their friends to their future employers. (All of the hands come down.) After dialogue about the shortcomings of their friends (tardiness, attitudes, etc.), I remind them they are already creating the impression of who they will be at work even before they get their first jobs. If your best friends won't hire you, who will? I advise them to be the person anyone would be proud to recommend."**

Be assertive about promoting yourself. You may feel desperate, but don't come off this way. Job hunting can be stressful, but the more confident you appear, the better impression you'll make.

Self-promotion can be accomplished tastefully; don't be afraid of coming across as opportunistic. Successful networking is essentially building relationships, and you should endeavor to help others at the same time you're hoping to make useful associations for yourself. But this self-selling concept can seem intimidating if you tend to be shy.

Keep in mind that just because you may be introverted, bashful, or not particularly a people person does not mean you're not entitled to a good job. You still need to learn to network, just practice with trusted friends before you venture out to less familiar people. If you're concerned about becoming sweaty or tongue-tied, role-play your pitch until you feel confident sharing your talents and skills.

Incidentally, even if you feel the need to practice your networking with friends, there's no need to prepare an elaborate speech in which you outline who you are and what you hope to do for a living. Break your pitch down to two minutes or less so you can utilize it at random moments when you bump into acquaintances at the mall or in the elevator in your apartment building. You can easily do this if you know the line of work you're looking for and can speak confidently about your abilities and objectives. If you can summarize your field of interest, your strengths or talents, how you can be reached, and the fact that you're a recent graduate who's looking for work, all in a two-minute span, you've got a worthy pitch! Make a strong impression on your networking contacts and let them know you're serious about your professional future.

You may also consider having business cards printed. These days, there are various online companies that offer cards for a few dollars or even offer them for free if you're okay with their advertising logo on the back (this is the least preferable option, but it still works). You can get glossy cards in a variety of colors (think professional, though) and just print your name, e-mail address, and phone number on them—you can also add your field. As you meet people, you can hand them a card to make it easier for them, or their contact, to get in touch with you.

**ADVICE FROM THE CORNER OFFICE**
Susan Sellani-Hosage, a senior manager in human resources, reminds: "The interviewer is not your friend, psychologist, or clergyman. Save any dialog that doesn't positively contribute to your candidacy for some other time. Your interview is your short, distinct window of opportunity to present only those skills and accomplishments that will get you the job. Use your time wisely."

### Pitching Style (not the Baseball Kind)

If you feel unsure about the correct networking approach, you may be surprised to learn that there really isn't just one foolproof method. The most effective approach is the one that works best for you, your personality type, and your comfort level. If you can conjure up an image of a savvy and successful networker, emulate this person's winning style and you'll be on your way to uncovering your best approach. At first you may feel as though you're role-playing, but soon you'll adopt a technique that feels natural. And the more you work on that technique, the better you'll get.

Remember, networking is a two-way street. While looking for help, consider how you might be able to help others. You may not know any corporate movers and shakers, but you may be able to give your contact some pointers on how her college-age son can make the school soccer team.

# CLASS NOTES

Brian, 25

Brian graduated with a computer science degree from USC at age twenty-one. He received numerous calls and secured several interviews from his efforts, but most job offers were on the East Coast and he wanted to stay in Southern California; he was determined to find a good position in his chosen field and location, no matter how long it took.

He took what he calls a "starter job" **while he pursued the position he really wanted** and soon received a call from a former professor who helped him get an interview with one of the Big Four accounting firms. He was hired and worked there more than fifteen months when he realized he wanted to have more of a hands-on position in his field of study.

He moved on to another job at a notable software company and imagined the work would be much more glamorous than it actually turned out to be. Long hours and less-than-challenging assignments **propelled him to seek different work** as a computer scientist. He again began networking and letting everyone he ran across know that he was job searching. He described his dream position and was booked for an interview with a financial asset company for a position he believed might be too good to be true. Now twenty-five years old, Brian has been with this company for more than a year building websites and designs for internal corporate use. He loves his job, receives great benefits, and hopes to work his way up the ranks.

An intelligent guy with confidence and charisma, Brian always felt that **building contacts was of more value** than getting good grades, although his scores were stellar. His word of advice to recent graduates looking for work: "Stay in touch with the students and professors you met in college because they can be a great resource. They know a lot of people and can help connect you to a great job opportunity."

Networking opportunities also extend beyond in-person occasions. In addition to making the most of your personal interactions, consider participating in networking websites and online discussion groups. There are thousands of these for almost every imaginable profession, and employers sometimes tune in to screen potential job candidates. Use Vault (*www.vault.com*) or Wetfeet.com's (*www.wetfeet.com*) message boards to get the inside scoop on career fields and employers of interest to you. E-mail is also a widely used and perfectly acceptable way to network, but you want to keep your message to the point and be sure to check your spelling and grammar.

## INFORMATIONAL INTERVIEWS

An informational interview is like a fact-finding tour. Setting up an informational interview is as easy as a quick e-mail or phone call to a prospective employer or someone in the field. You'll learn more about how to make contact in Chapter 5, but it consists of setting up a meeting with a professional in your particular field who will tell you about the company he or she works for and what some of the positions within that organization might entail. More managers, vice presidents, executives, and even employees who love their jobs are willing to meet with you than you think. People love talking about themselves, and you are looking for people to not only impart what they know but also to simply talk about themselves and their profession.

The most important thing is to go into informational interviews with a realistic outlook. Don't walk in thinking that the interviewer will hire you on the spot! You'll only leave disappointed. Use the time to gather information about the career, receive job advice and, above all, network. Remember, the person you are talking to may know a colleague at another company who is hiring or he or she may just be another good informational contact that could help you get a job down the road. Networking is all about getting in touch with as many people as possible, and you never know when someone will be able to help you out.

**ADVICE FROM THE CORNER OFFICE**
Keith Oreson, executive vice president of the *Fortune* 500 company Advance Auto Parts, Inc., suggests: "If you don't know what type of position you want, talk to people who are working in jobs of interest to you and find out what they do and how they got to the position. A lot of people love to talk and give insight. Another way to go about it is to target people in companies or industries of interest to you."

During the interview, take notes, dress as if it is a true job interview, and remember to genuinely thank the person for giving his or her time to help you out. (Incidentally, "please" and "thank you" are two valuable sentiments that will take you far in not only meeting people but in landing a job.) While people love talking, they still have to take care of responsibilities at work.

It's a good idea to prepare a list of questions to ask once you have an informational interview scheduled:

- What is a typical day like within this career field? What are typical challenges?
- Why does this field/work interest you? How did you get started?

- What suggestions do you have that can help me break into this field?
- What about your career within this field do you find the most rewarding?
- What don't you like about this field?
- Why did you choose to work for this company?
- Why do customers choose this company?
- What technological advances does this company utilize?
- What are the most important skills and/or strengths to be successful within this field?
- What is the culture of this company? Is it typical of most within this field?
- Does this field have a high turnover?
- Is there work/life balance within this field? This company?
- Would higher education help one to advance?
- Are you aware of any positions at this company for which I might be qualified?

This constructive critiquing is priceless . . . be open-minded and take it all in—it will only propel you to success!

**ADVICE FROM THE CORNER OFFICE**
Julie Grass, HR professional and founder of the Momentum Group, recommends: "Think about the questions you want to ask ahead of time so that you are respectful of the person's time and also hone in on those things you really care about. Often these are quality-of-life questions, such as "What kinds of things have you found most exciting about your work?" and, conversely, "What are the greatest stressors?"

## SEARCH THE WEB

Job search sites have become very streamlined. You can search the mainstream ones, but do some research on the customized boards within each career field. You can also look up the websites of companies you're interested in and check for their job or career links. There are countless online directories and services that can help job seekers with everything from preparing a resume to finding a perfect work match. Here are a few good ones, valid at the time of publication:

### *www.BilingualCareer.com*
If you speak English and at least one other language, you can search this free job-listing site and find useful interviewing and resume preparation advice.

### *www.CareerBuilder.com*
This is one of the nation's leading newspaper and job listing links. This free site also includes other valuable resources.

### *www.Career.com*
This easy-to-use site offers jobs searchable by company, location, and discipline. Bonus: a listing of jobs for new college grads!

### *www.CareerExposure.com*
Check career categories directly from a variety of corporate human resources web pages. Also offers tips about job hunting and career advancement.

### *www.Careerjournal.com*
This *Wall Street Journal* resource offers lots of job opportunities and great articles about applying for and getting the job you want.

### www.CollegeJobBoard.com

A great resource for students and college grads where they can find internship, full- or part-time work, search for scholarships, and find job search tips.

### www.EmploymentGuide.com

Search for jobs, post a resume, and find career advice on this handy site. This site also offers job listing for dozens of specific metropolitan areas, which is useful when geography has to be factored into the job hunt equation!

### www.Employment911.com

Review more than 350 major job sites and create an online resume that is posted to thousands of employers. Also includes tools, links, free e-mail accounts, and other great resources.

### www.GrassIsGreener.com

A listing of more than 7 million jobs from job boards and corporate sites. Includes resume posting and blasting services.

### www.HotJobs.com

One of the most well-known sites, searches are available for all industries in all states.

### www.Indeed.com

A job search site of more than 500 places on the web, including major job boards, newspapers, and career centers.

### www.Job.com

Search thousands of jobs by industry, city, state, or specific position.

### www.Jobbankinfo.org

There are nearly a million job leads on this site. Post your resume for free, too!

**www.JobCenterUSA.com**
Search for jobs by skills, location, industry, and experience.

**www.Jobcentral.com**
A national employment network to provide career opportunities in all levels and a variety of industries.

**www.JobGuru.com**
A general job site where you can post multiple versions of your resume and use a job-search agent.

**www.JobWarehouse.com**
Job hunters in the computer/high-tech field can post resumes, search openings, and use a search agent to find job matches.

**www.Monster.com**
Probably the most well-known job site on the web, with hundreds of thousands of jobs worldwide. Includes career articles and advice and relocation services for job seekers.

**www.MyCareerSpace.com**
Post up to five different resumes that you can then use to apply to job openings online. Also includes info on career expos, insurance, and more.

**www.NowHiring.com**
Post your resume and provide detailed information through an online interview!

**www.Prohire.com**
One of the largest job sites on the web, with more than 150,000 job listings worldwide.

**www.TopUSAJobs.com**
A job site that lists the top jobs from numerous industries and a range of locations.

# CLASS NOTES

Jane, 25

A graduate from Boston University in 2004, Jane has a BS in mathematics and economics. Right out of college she took a few months off to travel to Australia and then began to volunteer back in her hometown of Cleveland, helping inner-city kids complete their high school education. Prior to graduation she had posted her resume on Monster. com, and **during her volunteer stint** she received a call from one of the largest sports entertainment companies in the country.

She interviewed and was hired as a cash manager in the treasury department where she oversaw incoming and outgoing payments. Two years later she was promoted to the assistant treasury position where she gave first approval on payments and handled foreign currency trades and anything associated with financial inflow and outflow.

Well into her first career, Jane decided to move to the West Coast, but since she didn't know a soul, her job hunt proved challenging. "I started by designing a spreadsheet where I listed the companies I was interested in and started looking up names and numbers," she recalls. "**I talked to everyone** about the types of jobs I wanted—you'd be surprised how small the world is once you start conversation."

She used **other online and traditional job-search tools** as well. "I posted my resume on Monster.com and HotJobs.com," she explains. "And I contacted the alumni association at BU and started attending local alumni events." One of the connections she made at the alumni association knew someone who was looking to hire a financial analyst for a large golf equipment firm. Jane applied and was hired.

"The best career advice I ever received was from my father," she relays. "He believes **the twenties are all about learning what you want and what you don't**, and the first job only serves to set you on the path to uncovering the career you really want."

**www.USAJOBS.com**
Offers employment opportunities with the United States federal government. Also includes tips for finding work with the government.

### HERE ARE EVEN MORE:

- *www.careerjournal.com*
- *www.careerplanner.com*
- *www.computerjobs.com*
- *www.consumersearch.com*
- *www.dice.com*
- *www.FederalJobSearch.com*
- *www.job-hunt.org*
- *www.jobing.com*
- *www.jobfactory.com*

If you are looking for a job in a particular industry, for example graphic design, interior design, archaeology, etc., check the websites of the professional organizations associated with that industry for job postings related to that particular field.

## JOB FAIRS

Job fairs are excellent places to distribute your resume and make connections. Your alma mater may offer these to current students as well as to recent graduates. Check a local newspaper for listings as job fairs—either industry-specific job fairs or those sponsored by a particular company or organization—now take place frequently and in almost every corner of the United States.

Be sure to go equipped to the fair! Bring along a professional-looking folder to hold copies of your own resume, as well as a place to keep company information that you pick up at the various booths. Be sure to dress in a professional manner that reflects the position you hope to get. For instance, if you're attending a job fair for banking candidates, wear an appropriate suit. If the job fair is in the fashion industry or hair design field, show off your creative side (while still dressing tastefully, of course). Dress professionally, no matter what, even if the position you're after is less formal. It's always better to be overdressed, than under—you'd rather an employer give you permission to dress down than to have to ask you to dress more professionally.

**ADVICE FROM THE CORNER OFFICE**
**Dayle Dalton, vice president of human resources at Los Robles Hospital and Medical Center, believes you should attend job fairs because:**

- **You have the opportunity to learn a lot at one time rather than through a variety of separate appointments.**
- **You gain exposure and can sell yourself as a person. It's one thing to look good on a resume, but as an applicant you want to sell your personality, your caring and passionate attitude.**
- **The HR staff and department directors are usually on hand to review applications, interview candidates, and answer questions.**

## THE ALUMNI ADVANTAGE

As a job applicant, the fact that you're a college graduate is a huge advantage, not only because you're more qualified than your undereducated peers, but because of the ongoing support most universities extend to their graduates. Many companies regularly call on alumni of particular universities to fill open positions. Participate in your alumni group to take advantage of these valuable connections.

Many colleges provide services that include chapters and career events where you can mix, mingle, and network. Some universities offer mentoring programs and provide a directory of resources that you can utilize to gather information about prospective employers. Your college may also have a social networking platform where you can connect with professionals, recent graduates, and others who can help you land the job you want. This information should be readily available on your college or university's homepage.

## VOLUNTEER

You'll find plenty of opportunities to network when you volunteer for positions in your area of interest. Volunteering is a great way to gain visibility and develop relationships—especially for the less assertive job seeker—as it allows you to show off your skills to people who may have professional connections. If you're a great event coordinator, help arrange fundraisers and banquets. You'll gain noticeable exposure while you help a needy organization, and make networking connections.

## PARTICIPATE IN A SEMINAR OR GROUP

Seminars and conferences are also great places to gain exposure. Check your local newspaper or specific corporate websites for leads and details. Register to attend the ones in your field of interest, and be sure to accept invitations to volunteer or participate in the various activities offered. Investment corporations, local schools, hospitals, computer companies, and a host of other fields will frequently host such events.

In addition to attending seminars, join as groups since these offer opportunities to make contacts and help you achieve personal growth. If you love to dance, join a dance group. Love to sing? Join a choir. How about a theater club, a political discussion forum, a book club, wine club—any collection of people who love to do what you do will work. You'll meet others with similar interests who are probably also wired to network.

Accept party invitations and attend engagements with the goal of making new connections. When appropriate, casually mention to your new acquaintances that you are seeking employment. Accept all the invitations you receive—you never know where or when you may meet the person who will help you find the job you seek.

## JOIN A CAREER GROUP

You may also want to participate in career groups such as the Five O'Clock Club (*www.fiveoclockclub.com*). This membership organization offers career-coaching and job-placement assistance, as well as weekly meetings and networking opportunities. With branches in Manhattan, Washington, D.C., and Chicago, this group provides an information exchange offering referrals to contacts in specific industries and lectures led by career coaches. They also hold discussion sessions where participants practice their two-minute pitches in small groups, which is of great value in a job hunt.

Also, as there is so much communication involved in a job search, you may want to participate in organizations designed to help improve your speaking skills. The Dale Carnegie schools (*www.dalecarnegie.com*) and Toastmasters (*www.toastmasters.org*) are leaders in promoting personal confidence, networking, and communication. They have great track records with students and professionals, prominent reputations, and result-oriented programs that will help you prepare for your interviews.

**STAY WITH IT**

Don't be discouraged if your initial contacts don't pan out. If someone declares that she simply doesn't have any ideas or connections for you, ask if she knows someone who might. Don't forget to send the all-important thank-you note if someone extends you a hand or has given you any of their time during your job search. The contact may prove valuable at a later date, and courtesy is always remembered. An e-mail thank-you note is perfectly acceptable. Also, if you're given a lead that proves to be valuable, call your contact source and let him or her know how your meeting, introduction, or interview went, and be sure to thank your contact source for the referral. ■

## cheat sheet

Do be prepared when you go to a job fair; bring resumes and dress professionally.

Don't forget to send a thank-you note when someone helps you in any way.

Don't ask for a job; ask for advice instead.

Don't be afraid to talk to people anywhere about your goals and needs, or to ask for connections.

Don't underestimate the value of joining groups and networking.

Don't skip the steps of networking, informational interviews, and making contacts.

## CHAPTER 4

# First Things First

## CRAFTING A RESUME AND COVER LETTER

> "If you don't tell people about your success, they probably won't know about it."
>
> DONALD TRUMP

Your resume—an extremely important piece of correspondence—is a true first impression. Recruiters read this piece of paper without seeing what you look like or having the opportunity to be charmed by your personality and listen to your witty, educated answers. An HR manager will often receive at least ten resumes a day for a posted position, and your resume can even end up in a stack of fifty or more. These managers scan resumes and quickly decide which candidates will advance. To stand out from the pack, make sure your resume is concise, packed with valuable and relevant information, and is easy to read. Consider your resume as a ticketed invite to an interview, and make sure it communicates the best you possible.

This chapter details how to write a winning resume—or if you've already written it, what pieces to double-check. We talked with HR professionals and will give you advice and quotes as to what they specifically look for when a resume lands on their desk.

Before getting into the how-tos, the basics must be stressed first: you *must* write a resume using proper grammar and spelling. Even though many have had these rules drilled into their heads, it is amazing how many resumes show up on the desks of human resource professionals with easy-to-spot errors. A good rule of thumb is this: after you write your resume (following the steps in the next section), leave it for a day and then reread it. Chances are you will find something to change. Once you feel comfortable, give it to at least three people to see if they catch any errors. This is very important because many managers will toss a resume with errors straight into the garbage. If you send in a poorly written resume, the potential employer will wonder what kind of correspondence you would someday send out to clients and vendors. Don't take the basics for granted—and be sure to proofread.

**ADVICE FROM THE CORNER OFFICE**
**Keith Oreson, executive vice president of the *Fortune* 500 company Advance Auto Parts, Inc., says, "These days, between spellcheck, books on how to write a resume, the Internet, and plain old common sense, there's no excuse to have misspelled words or a sloppy resume. To have a mistake is a negative comment on someone's thought process."**

## BRAINSTORM AND BEGIN

When you begin writing your resume, you want to list out every achievement, award, recognition, and idea that you've ever had, facilitated, created, executed, or handled. Some of these you may have already put on paper when you made your personal and professional inventory list in Chapter 2, but if necessary, keep brainstorming; keep writing. Put it ALL out there. You'll edit later on paper, but for now, don't edit in your mind because once your ideas are out there in written form, you may realize they really do belong on your resume.

**ADVICE FROM THE CORNER OFFICE**
Keith Oreson, executive vice president of the *Fortune* 500 company Advance Auto Parts, Inc., recommends showing progress in responsibilities across internships, positions, and projects. Give specifics on accomplishments to show a natural progression of leadership and movement. Quantifying your results will further reinforce your successes.

This brainstorming session should also include every committee you've ever served on, every job or internship you've held, and every volunteer event of which you've been a part. Focus on your achievements, not just your job duties. Depending on the amount or type of your experience, you may have to be creative when pulling out achievements from these positions. Or you may find out that you have so much more experience than you even thought you had. But list, list, list, and sort it out later. Write down achievements from the following:

- Internships
- Work-study jobs
- Study-abroad experiences
- Career shadowing

- Certifications received
- Summer positions
- Entrepreneurial ventures
- Temp work completed
- Sports participation
- Volunteer work (campus, church, clubs, community)
- Additional research or projects completed outside of a required class
- Greek (fraternity, sorority) leadership positions
- Student government positions

## TELL A TRUTHFUL STORY

As tempting as it is to exaggerate your accomplishments, don't! The story you tell needs to be yours, and it must be true and real. Restrain yourself. Embellishment may get you in the door, but it will come back to haunt you. It will either trip you up in the interview or, worse, get you fired after hiring if/when the truth comes out. Although you want to avoid exaggeration on your resume, you still want to get *your* story across to the interviewer.

**ADVICE FROM THE CORNER OFFICE**
La'Trise Smith, assistant vice president of human resources at Huntington Bank, says applicants need to tell the story of what they want and why. "It is as simple as starting your resume with a career objective. Tell me what you're looking for and then the rest of the resume needs to tell me why you're qualified to fill the position."

## WRITING THE OBJECTIVE

Including an objective on a resume wasn't always necessary, but now almost every professional recruiter we've spoken to says the objective is of the utmost importance. It should go right at the top of the resume and should, in fact, be the very first line.

When interviewers look at your resume, they want to see a solidified career objective. Avoid generic statements such as "To obtain a full-time job with a company providing growth and challenge." There are hundreds of companies offering growth and challenge—including the bike shop on the corner. Set yourself apart from your competition by knowing what you want and communicating this information to your prospective interviewer. Try to stay away from the words "allowing me" or "utilizing" because everyone uses them and they seem uninspired. Instead, consider *apply, contribute, pursue, develop,* or *providing the opportunity.*

Be careful of adding the tag line "that provides growth and experience." You don't want employers to think that you are just looking for a stepping-stone job—that you are only going to use them to gain experience. Employers want to believe you will contribute to the company just as much as (if not more than) they will contribute to helping you build your experience portfolio.

If you are responding to an advertisement specifically stating that the position provides growth, then by all means add the line. You want employers to know you want growth, and the fact the position offers it should be recognized.

When writing your objective, state a specific career field or a specific position, and absolutely spell out your strongest qualifications. A good formula to use is: A position {insert particular position or a particular field} where I can use my {insert qualifications}.

For example:

- *A position in the IT department where I can apply and contribute my computer troubleshooting experience and skills.*
- *A position as a social worker giving me the opportunity to use my education and experience to help children and families in troubled situations.*

## A QUICK SUMMARY

After the objective, give a brief summary of your qualifications, either in bullet points or italicized to set them off from the objective. Examples:

*Professional . . . Talented . . .Creative . . . Computer and AutoCAD literate . . . Team player . . . Strong communication skills . . . Work well with people at all levels and diversity backgrounds*

- More than two years of progressive computer programming and troubleshooting experience.
- Computer internship with [insert company] in [insert city].
- Graduated cum laude with BS in computer science.
- Computer literate; proficient in [insert all known programs].

Then tell the employer about your education:

Bachelor of Science in Engineering, Date
Purdue University, West Lafayette, Indiana
Magna Cum Laude; 3.9 G.P.A. on 4.0 scale

An option here is to also insert coursework you have taken relevant to the position requested. Your education information can either be at the beginning or end of your resume.

## FORMATTING THE STORY

Next comes listing your achievements with bullet points. You'll probably hear many different opinions on how to categorize your achievements. You can choose to organize either by skill sets or by places of employment. The key is to look at your brainstorming list and see what style works best for you. With your limited experience up to this point, determine which option is more feasible for your particular situation. You want to present the best possible resume—not whatever style is trendy.

If you choose skill set grouping, you can list achievements under headings such as Leadership, Team Participation, Communication, Computer Skills, Organization, Trade Skills (design, IT, marketing, whatever your field), Research, and Management. For example, under Organization, list all the projects you've been responsible for organizing at both employment positions and campus clubs. Examples:

LEADERSHIP
- Facilitated {insert action} at {insert where}.
- Initiated {insert action} at {insert where}.
- Coordinated {insert action} at {insert where}.

COMMUNICATION
- Created and wrote {insert what} at {insert where}.
- Presented policies to more than 100 employees at company meeting for {insert company}.

Get the idea? You can also list by tasks within the field. For example, within the Trade Skills (accounting) field: Accounts Receivable, Accounts Payable, and Payroll.

If it makes more sense to you to list your skills by company, include the company name, position, city, and dates:

**ERNST AND YOUNG, Chicago, IL**
*Internship, September 2008 to May 2009*

- list achievement (or responsibility, duty) and outcome
- list achievement and outcome
- list achievement and outcome

Whenever possible, include an outcome. Example:

- Co-faciliated a project distributed to a potential new client; client signed a one-year contract.
- Organized a new, color-coded filing system for front office; the entire office implemented the system.

If you choose the skill-set option, be sure to create a separate section to indicate which companies you worked for during what time periods to clarify employment history. If you choose to list achievements by employer, then you want to present the most relevant activities to demonstrate all you have achieved during the course of your employment history.

## ACTION VERBS

No matter what style you choose, be sure to start your sentences with an action or power verb. These are verbs that make an immediate impact in a short span of time. Seems easy, right? Many resumes, however, aren't consistent throughout. They'll switch and start a sentence with "Responsible for . . . " or "Responsibilities included . . . " Be sure every sentence consistently starts with a power verb.

Be creative and think of true action verbs. The verbs *worked on* or *managed* don't carry the excitement that *launched* or *compiled* do. There are, of course, some great standbys such as *created, facilitated,* and *coordinated.* Just be sure that the whole sentence packs a punch.

## NO LINGO

Avoid industry lingo. Sometimes companies use outside recruiters who don't understand the terminology and may overlook you as a qualified, excellent candidate. Ask someone who is not in your career field about the word and see if the average person recognizes the term. Remember, it's always better to err on the side of universal, professional language.

## QUANTIFY

Whenever possible and applicable, quantify why what you did is so important: "Launched a program for student government to increase fundraising dollars" isn't as powerful as "Launched a program for student government to increase fundraising dollars resulting in an increase of $1,500 from prior semester."

By putting exact dollar amounts, you show that you not only know the value of your contributions but you also offer specifics of what you could possibly do for your prospective company.

You can explain how you did it during the interview; on the resume, just give the facts.

## WHAT ELSE DO YOU LIKE?

Employers want to see a well-rounded candidate. If you're an avid marathon runner or in an intramural soccer league, add this at the bottom of your resume. You want it to show off a little bit of your personality, too.

You may think running the marathon every year is either just your own personal triumph or something you do for fun, but in reality most people understand the discipline it takes to train for one. This says a great deal about your dedication, discipline, and ability to commit to a challenge—traits your interviewer hopes to see you bring to a position. It also helps add more qualities to your personality, since you are a new grad, and your professional experience is most likely limited.

## MORE THAN ONE RESUME

You will probably have more than one resume because you may be applying for more than one type of job or more than one job title. You'll obviously only send applicable resumes to respective positions. If your career goals provide flexibility within a given field, the resume needs to be tailored to a specific position.

And remember to ask several people to proofread it. There shouldn't be any spelling errors, and all verbs should be in the correct tense. Also ask the proofreaders to ensure as many statements/achievements as possible are quantified, using details to demonstrate how you did it. A resume with errors will rarely make it to an interviewer's desk.

Let's look at some sample resumes on the following pages. Included are:

*A bad resume and ways to improve it.*
PAGE 54

*A good resume and why it is an improvement over the bad resume.*
PAGE 57

*A decent resume and why it is not a good resume.*
PAGE 61

*A good resume and what makes it good.*
PAGE 64

*A good skill-based resume and why it works.*
PAGE 69

## cheat sheet

Don't make your resume more than two pages; right out of college, it will most likely be one page.

Do make sure your resume is grammatically correct and free of typos.

Do make sure at least three people proof your resume before you send it out.

Don't include a picture.

Do only include positions or activities relevant to the career you're pursuing.

Don't embellish (or lie).

Don't use industry lingo.

Do include results when applicable.

**A Bad Resume:**

# JENNIFER JOHNSON

17600 Massey Avenue • Oak Park, Ca, 91377
Home: 555.555.5555 • Cell: 555.555.5554
E-mail: HiJennny@yahoo.com (note the three Ns)

**OBJECTIVE:** To obtain postproduction position in a creative media environment.

**EDUCATION**
**Bachelor of Arts • Film and Visual Culture**
**University of California Riverside • 2006**
*Dean's List • (Finished college in 3 years)*
Emphasis: comprehensive coverage in film and media studies, critical theory, non-Hollywood cinema and media forms, experimental film, and production.

**Education Abroad Program • August–December 2005**
Lived with a French family in Lyon, France, for a semester while attending the University of Lyon. Attended an intensive language immersion program at the intermediate level designed to improve oral and written language skills while providing a foundation in French culture and society. All courses were taught in the French language.

**EXPERIENCE**
**Pasadena Academy of Performing Arts • 2007–Present**
*Production Assistant*
Assist the artistic director with administrative, creative, and potential clients.

75 W. Bellmont Ave. • Pasadena, Ca, 91105 • 626.768.2614

**Big Sports Productions • 2006–2007**
*Production Assistant*
Logging, editing, digitizing, and dubbing on Avid system in the professional sports market.

892 Washington Rd. • Westlake Village, Ca, 91361 • (555) 555-5555

**Big Sports Productions • 2005–2006**
*Unpaid internship/school credit*
Basics of editing, html, and web design.

892 Washington Rd. • Westlake Village, Ca, 91361 • (555) 555-5555

**Personal Assistant to Gary and Dinnah Grayborn • 2003–2005**
*Did personal and professional things for the Grayborns.*

**Barnes and Noble • 2002–2003**
*Sales Associate • Music Department*

270 Fourth Ave. • Westlake Village, Ca, 91361 • (805) 446-2820

**Oncology Medical Center • 2000–2002**
*Health Care Assistant*
Assisted in an oncology office serving the needs of chemotherapy patients.

Dr. Harold Killinger • 689 Encino Rd. #25 • Los Angeles, 93065 • (805) 555-5555

**SKILLS**
Photoshop, Illustrator (basic), Final Cut Pro, Flash (basic), Dreamweaver (basic)

Photography, Conceptual Video Art

Microsoft Word, Excel, Features Writing, Essay Writing

Some reasons why this is a bad resume:

➤ Nothing is explained. And there is so much here to expand upon!

➤ The objective is generic and doesn't really explain anything about what she is really looking to contribute.

➤ There should be a section summing up her additional qualities.

➤ She doesn't explain what she did for each position. There are probably many exciting projects she contributed to at Big Sports Productions—especially if she worked on pro sports accounts—so what did she do for them? What did the editing consist of?

➤ The sales associate position—there is so much opportunity to show qualifications worthy to the potential employer. Did she win any contests? Did she ever receive top sales for the day? Was the art of persuasion needed?

➤ Her e-mail address is too confusing. If you have to indicate there are "three Ns," the e-mail address is too confusing. Create a new e-mail address that portrays a more professional image.

➤ It most likely takes a special kind of person to work in an oncology center. What traits helped her be successful there for two years?

See how much potential there is to expand on this resume?

## A Good Resume

Here is one way to make the bad resume more presentable:

---

### JENNIFER JOHNSON

1609 Morris Way • Westlake Village, Ca, 91361
Home: 555.555.5555 • Cell: 555.555.5554
E-mail: Jennifer.Johnson@mac.com

**OBJECTIVE:** To be actively involved in the artistic and administrative process of creating and assembling mixed-media forms, from production to postproduction.

**SUMMARY:** creative . . . artistic . . . software proficient . . . motivated . . . hardworking . . . talented

**EDUCATION**
**Bachelor of Arts: Film and Visual Culture, University of California Riverside, 2006**
*Dean's List; finished college in 3 years*

Comprehensive coverage in:
• Film and media studies
• Critical theory
• Hollywood and non-Hollywood cinema
• History of experimental cinema and media forms
• Studies included research in cinema beyond the economic, institutional, and aesthetics of mainstream film production

**Education Abroad Program, August to December 2005**
Lived with a French family in Lyon, France, for a semester. Attended the University of Lyon in an intensive language immersion program at the intermediate level. Improved oral and written language skills while experiencing a foundation in French culture and society. All courses were taught in the French language.

**EXPERIENCE**

**Pasadena Academy of Performing Arts**

75 W. Bellmont Ave., Pasadena, CA; 626.768.2614; 2007 to present

*Production Assistant*

- Execute the visions of the Artistic Director in both administrative and creative details
- Manage construction and remodel process
- Supervise design process within company's fixed budget
- Schedule and coordinate interviews with potential clients
- Solve concerns of employees and interested clients
- Develop advertising ideas and distribution
- Facilitate office work: Write letters and e-mails to clients and colleagues, heavy phone use, use and install PC computers, and tend to the organization of the studio

**Big Sports Productions**

892 Washington Rd., Westlake Village, CA; 555.555.5555; 2006 to 2007

*Production Assistant and Receptionist; completed internship 2005–2006*

- Provided administrative and technical assistance to the executive director and staff
- Prepared basic audio/video concepts and configurations for editors
- Logged, edited, digitized, and dubbed on Avid
- Managed time and prioritized assignments for personnel
- Organized deliveries and receivables
- Facilitated office work: scanned photos and edited in Photoshop, heavy Internet research for various projects, created DVDs and labels, sent mail via FedEx, restocked office supplies, organized filing system, ran errands, and, when needed, stayed well after hours to assist colleagues in completing projects

- Interned to learn how to edit and design websites with HTML coding

**Personal Assistant to Gary and Dinnah Grayborn**

2003–2005

_Assisted Gary and Dinnah Grayborn (Line Producer and Costume Designer)_

- Organized daily priorities for the Grayborns
- Tended to the cleanliness of work and living space
- Assisted in various personal needs
- Ran errands, made important deliveries and pickups, and occasionally assisted on location during the filmmaking process

**Oncology Medical Center**

Dr. Harold Killinger, 689 Encino Rd. #25, Los Angeles, CA; 805.555.5555; 2000 to 2002

_Health Care Assistant_

- Assisted patients during chemotherapy treatments in an oncology office, tending to their immediate physical and emotional needs

**SKILLS**

- Photoshop
- Final Cut Pro
- Mac proficient
- Digitizing/Logging on Avid
- Dreamweaver and Flash Basic
- Conceptual Video Art, Features and Essay Writing
- Microsoft Word, ExcelBetty Moviyna

Some reasons why this is an improved resume:

- ➤ Every sentence is bulleted and starts with an action verb.
- ➤ More information is given for a clearer picture of what she did at each job.
- ➤ There is a concise objective and a summary included at the top of the resume.
- ➤ She used a more professional e-mail address.
- ➤ The Barnes & Noble position was removed after further review because there were no specialties that she could include.

This resume could be even better if results were included, but only if they are real and applicable.

## A Decent Resume:

Betty Moviyna
Betty1@mac.com • 555.555.5555
12409 Fullerton Ave., #5, Santa Monica, CA

**OBJECTIVE:** To obtain a position as a talent coordinator in a creative environment.

**EMPLOYMENT:**
*Talent Coordinator,* **Romano Klutky Talent,** 2003–Present

- Review art portfolios and prepare them for further consideration
- Responsible for providing tours of the studio
- Source and screen candidates with the director of recruitment
- Support executives by coordinating domestic and international travel arrangements
- Organize meetings, corporate events, and oversee all details on site
- Prepare materials for presentations and lectures
- Administer artists' database using FileMaker Pro
- Manage Mr. Klutky's busy calendar
- Assist with various administrative duties and general office organization
- Screen calls and handle company guests prior to their scheduled meetings
- Compose letters and documents on behalf of the president
- Oversee market research for animation magazines and articles

*Executive Administrative Assistant,*
**Fun Animation Animated Studio,** 2001–2003

- Supported and assisted the Director of Artistic Recruitment
- Coordinated domestic and international travel arrangements
- Oversaw the flow of incoming/outgoing portfolios and demo reels
- Managed the front office while providing administrative support
- Coordinated speaking engagements, business trips, and special events
- Screened calls and handled company guests prior to their scheduled meetings
- Corresponded with potential candidates prior to interviewing

**EDUCATION:**
UCLA Extension, Los Angeles, CA – *Visual Arts/ Computer Graphics Certification Program*

Santa Monica College, Santa Monica, CA

**APPLICABLE SOFTWARE:**
PC/Mac Platforms, Microsoft Office (Word, Excel, Outlook), FileMaker Pro, Act, Illustrator

Some reasons why this is a decent resume (but not good):

- The objective is still pretty vague. Why a talent coordinator and why is a creative environment desired? The objective should be more thorough.
- There is a sentence starting with "Responsible" rather than an action verb; watch consistency.
- More explanation is needed for more punch: "Managed Mr. Klutky's busy calendar" could be "Managed Mr. Klutky's busy calendar to schedule travel, business meetings, movie still approvals, interviews, and designer appointments."
- It would be wise to consider organizing this resume with headings versus organizing by company.

# SALLY KROUPILOS

18106 Moniakia Lake Dr., Wheaton, IL 60477
708.555.5555/708.555.5555
sallykroupilos@aol.com

## DESIGNER OF LANDSCAPE AND INTERIOR SPACE PLANNING

**OBJECTIVE:** A position with a design firm where I am able to contribute with landscape and interior space planning creativity, providing residential or commercial spaces to satisfied customers.

**SUMMARY:** *Professional . . . Talented . . . Creative . . . Computer and AutoCAD literate . . . Team player . . . Strong communication skills . . . Work well with people at all levels and diversity backgrounds*

## SIGNIFICANT DESIGN ACCOMPLISHMENTS

*Perry, Johnson, and Maliachi Design; Internship; 09/2006 to 12/2007*

**932 Walnut Lane, Villa Park, IL; 09/2006**

- Designed coordinating color scheme for first floor and basement area.
- Designed banquette, with coordinating valance, for corner of kitchen to be used with existing table and chairs. Created more space for entertaining.
- Designed new vanities in bathroom with colors and tones to complement existing fixtures resulting in cost saving. Made selection of new faucets and fixtures. Chose decorative paint treatment for master bath.

- Chose new color scheme for basement; removed wallpaper and painted trim and outdated panels.
- Designed landscape border of evergreen, deciduous shrubs, and perennials. Disguised unsightly storage shed and telephone pole.

**1619 Oliver Road, Chicago, IL; 03/2007**
- Assisted in layout of bathroom remodel; chose color and tiles.
- Consulted for conversion of garage to home office: layout, colors, flooring, and location of doors, windows, and closets.
- Sketched preliminary design for future renovations.

**331 Sunset Lane, Sunnyside, IL; 04/2007**
- Consulted on window treatments for kitchen and dining areas.
- Provided ideas for decorative painting options for fireplace area.

**18209 Surrey Lake Drive, Tinley Park, IL; 12/2007**
- Managed remodel of kitchen, master bath, first floor.
- Managed home office and laundry center construction.

**9078 183rd Street, Frankfurt, IL; 11/2007**
- Consulted on landscape project; solved problem of unsightly underside of deck.
- Paved stable walk path.
- Added water feature; designed retaining wall with landscape feature near front easement.
- Designed and installed planting features and garden beds.
- Provided general management over project through completion.

## SCHOOL EXPERIENCE

**Levin House Project; 02/2006**

- Updated architecturally historic interior while maintaining design integrity.
- Selected furniture, chose materials and custom cabinetry design for placement.
- Created presentation with fully colored floor plan with furniture, black-and-white photocopies of furniture selections, sample board of material selections, colored cross-section elevation of main living spaces, and elevations of custom cabinets and design work.

**333 Wacker Building; 04/2006**

- Carved out, designed office space for fictional wood supply company within a desired amount of existing space.
- Designed space planning of area and offices, including furniture selection and placement, material selection, custom cabinetry design work, and custom woodwork.
- Created presentation of fully rendered and colored floor plan; designed fully colored renderings of custom design work within given space.

**Custom Residential Project; 05/2003**

- Designed custom floor plan, meeting specific requirements and needs of fictional family.
- Designed 3 bedrooms, 2.5 baths, library and media rooms, master suite, great room, dining and kitchen areas.
- Created presentation of original and custom space planning with fully rendered floor plan; full rendering in color of main living area, custom staircase, elevations of custom cabinetry. Designed kitchen, materials and furniture selection boards, and interior and exterior features for inclusion.

## ADDITIONAL ACCOMPLISHMENTS

**Crisis Center for Northern Suburbia; Northbrook, IL; 1997–2002**

*Volunteered at crisis hotline*

- Demonstrated ability to appropriately handle crises while answering calls needing immediate attention and discernment; provided information regarding specific circumstances.
- Assisted domestic abuse victims seeking emergency shelter, orders of protection, and guidance.
- Took potential suicide calls; listened, empathized, and calmed caller while tracing the call for police to respond.
- Completed intake forms for shelter guests; situated new residents with necessities; provided tour of the facilities and schedule of activities, rules, and regulations.
- Kept accurate documentation of all information.

## EDUCATION

- Harrington College of Design; graduated June 2006
- University of Illinois Extension; Master Gardener Series; completed March 2006
- Moriane Community College; 2004–2005
- Former member ASID student chapter

Some reasons why this is a good resume:

- The objective is clear and thorough.
- The summary is easy to read and to the point.
- Each project is spelled out and easy to understand.
- Items are bulleted.
- School experience included is relevant, categorized in a separate, organized area, and remains consistent with the objective.
- Overall, it is a clean, professional resume.

# DENISE RUSSELL

1146 Stanford #6, New York, NY    847.456.8413    denise55@yahoo.com

## OBJECTIVE

A position in human resources where I can contribute to training employees and building team environments.

## SUMMARY

Recruiting . . . Training & Development . . . Employee Relations . . . Excellent Communication Skills

## EDUCATION

Bachelor of Arts in Communication, May 2007
Indiana University, Bloomington, Indiana

Magna Cum Laude; 3.9 G.P.A. on 4.0 scale

## BUSINESS EXPERIENCE

Jonathan's Nursery; Indianapolis, IN
Internship 9/07 to 12/07
*Jonathan's Nursery is a leader in lawn and garden products, operating 170 stores within 14 states.*

Van Murray Department Store; Indianapolis, IN
Internship 1/07 to 4/07
*Van Murray is a specialty boutique-type department store located in the Indianapolis area.*

## SIGNIFICANT ACCOMPLISHMENTS

### RECRUITMENT

*Jonathan's:*

* Assisted in recruiting candidates within 90 stores for roll out of new corporate-wide program.
* Maintained chart logs for internal talent and external candidate pool for succession planning.
* Coordinated and participated, in conjunction with human resources manager, working with district managers in recruiting and hiring all store management.
* Created spreadsheets to strategically plan, chart, and track employee and management turnover.

*Van Murray:*

* Co-designed and implemented extensive interview process for the region via participation in task groups consisting of 8 human resources professionals.
* Offered suggestions to strengthen future intern programs consisting of selection process, seminars, meetings, and training sessions.

### EMPLOYEE CHAMPION

*Both Jonathan's and Van Murray:*

* Resolved employee issues: performance, harassment, discrimination, and sexual harassment allegations. Ensured legal compliance.
* Assisted in ongoing recognition programs for employees.

TRAINING AND DEVELOPMENT

*Jonathan's:*
- Participated in the creation and facilitation of leadership training for six district managers.
- Created companywide sexual harassment brochure.
- Co-initiated Diversity in the Workplace program.

*Van Murray:*
- Created and facilitated training and development sessions to educate on company practices, diversity awareness, harassment, and improving employee performance.
- Participated in creation of region's new-hire orientation training consisting of full day of activities.

**ADDITIONAL EDUCATION**

Creative Training Techniques, Patton Boggs Investigation Seminar, Legal training seminars; SHRM Diversity in the Workplace conference, Human Resources school coursework

**ASSOCIATIONS**

Society for Human Resource Management; student member

**COMMUNITY INVOLVEMENT**

Participated in Martin Luther King Jr. Day volunteer activities with Chicago Cares organization

Volunteer at Joshua House, a shelter for women in Chicago

**PERSONAL ACHIEVEMENTS**

Trained for and ran the Chicago Marathon 2004–2008

Some reasons why this is a good resume:

- This resume is all about HR experience so it makes sense to group it by headings, rather than company, which makes it more concise and easier to read.
- The summary is easy to read and to the point.
- Items are bulleted.
- Overall, it is a clean, professional resume.

## COVER LETTERS

Don't neglect the cover letter! A cover letter is not optional (even if the ad to which you are responding to indicates it is), nor is it separate; it is a complement to your resume. It introduces you to the hiring manager in a more personable way—meaning you actually create a sentence-structure communication with this person. Consider it your elevator speech on paper. (An elevator speech is your thirty-second introduction to someone about yourself when you only have a few floors in which to do so.)

In your cover letter, introduce yourself and explain why you are perfect for the job. Remember, your cover letter should support your resume, not reiterate it word for word. Pull out specific pieces from your resume to highlight the matching qualifications of the particular position you are seeking. If you're answering an advertisement with clarified requirements, use this to your advantage and match up exactly what they request with what you possess. Spell out your qualifications for them in no uncertain terms.

### COVER LETTER TIPS

1. Whenever possible, address your cover letter to someone in the company (the head of HR, the head of the department you're interviewing for) to make it more personal and professional. If this is not possible, address it to: Dear Hiring Professional.

2. Individualize each letter. Don't use a generic template; instead, pull out specific pieces of your resume that are custom-tailored for the specific job. This is time-consuming, but it will present your attention to detail to the hiring company.

3. Use proper grammar, and be error- and typo-free.

4. Use professional language. Avoid slang, jargon, and a casual tone.

5. Mention any achievements and awards that are relevant to the field or position to which you are applying.

6. Have a strong closing. State that you will follow up and then do it.

Have at least two people proofread your letter(s). Leave it alone for a day and then proofread it again before you send it to ensure it is completely error free.

Following are two example of cover letters. One is an example of a bad cover letter and the other is an example of a good cover letter.

# A Bad Cover Letter

To whom it may concern:

I have been employed as a talent recruiter at Belinda Smith Talent for the four years I've been in college and I have a vast interest and knowledge in the field of electronic art. I started as an intern.

Ms. Smith's experience as a recruiter spans over a decade as she has worked for companies such as Sony, Paramount, and Dreamworks. I began working with her as an executive assistant at Paramount where she was the director of artistic recruitment. At that point, we were crewing two movies and four television series and we learned to work well together from the start. Ms. Smith soon learned to rely on me as her "screening" person, as she simply did not have time to look at every portfolio or reel that came into our department.

For the past two years I have been working with Ms. Smith as a talent recruiter for her own company, which services studios worldwide in the crewing of visual effects and animation for film, television and commercials. She is now is in the process of moving the head office to Chicago and unfortunately I need to stay in the Los Angeles area. Needless to say, I consider this a huge loss as we have worked extremely well together for so many years and on so many levels.

Now I am seeking a career in which I can foster the same kind of productive experience as I have grown to appreciate working with Ms. Smith. I have a great admiration for your organization and have long thought that it would be an ideal place to apply my talents and skills. I would love the opportunity to speak with you about the idea of working for your company as a talent coordinator. I have attached my resume for your review; If you have any questions or wish to speak with me further, please feel free to contact me.

Sincerely,

Susie Jones
Talent Coordinator
Belinda Smith Talent
1234 California Ave, #5
Los Angeles, CA 90403
555.555.5555
susie@mac.com

Some reasons why this is bad cover letter:

- The grammar is terrible.
- Paragraphs are too long.
- Its not addressed to a particular individual—there was no research on the writer's part.
- The writer's address and contact info is buried at the bottom.
- The letter is all about Ms. Smith—where she worked, why she is moving, and so on. Also, the writer is basically saying that no job will be as good as working with Ms. Smith and her agency, but she'll give it a go since she has no choice as Ms. Smith is moving.

Susie Jones
1234 California Ave. #5, Los Angeles, CA 98765
555.555.5555
Susie@mac.com

Ms. Jennifer Popper
Fox Animated
5668 Main St.
Burbank, CA 12345

To Ms. Popper:

To have a successful animated project, it takes the right creative person for the job. As a talent coordinator, I can ensure Fox Animated recruits the most creative animators possible.

Working for more than four years, which started as an internship, with respected recruiter Belinda Smith, I possess exceptional knowledge within the field of electronic art. Responsible for screening animators for Ms. Smith, I have assisted in staffing for movies, television series, and commercials.

The company, Belinda Smith Animators, is now is in the process of relocating to Chicago. Having recently finished my degree, I am now seeking a full-time position within the Los Angeles area.

In addition to the skills of being able to recognize talent within the field of animation, I also possess skills of professionalism, follow-through, and sense of urgency and work well with people at all levels within an organization.

I have a great admiration for Fox Animated and know I can contribute to your team. I would like to speak with you about the opportunity to work for the company as a talent coordinator.

I can be reached at 555.555.5555 at any time. I will also follow up on receipt of my resume by the end of next week. I look forward to talking with you.

Sincerely,

Susie Jones

Some reasons why this is a good cover letter:

- It starts with a sentence about the field and mentions the company to which the writer is applying.
- The sentences are shorter and more concise.
- The experience is about Susie, not Belinda.

It really does make a difference what your resume and cover letter look like. This is your first impression the potential employer will have of you, and it communicates far more than you can imagine. You want to send out polished, professional correspondence demonstrating that you are polished and professional. Definitely invest the time in this beginning stage of the job search; it will lead you to the interviews. ■

## cheat sheet

Do send a cover letter with your resume.

Don't use a generic greeting if you can find the name of a specific person.

Don't use a sexist greeting ("Gentlemen").

Don't send the same letter to every employer; customize each letter.

Do be short and concise; don't use run-on sentences.

Do proof your letter *several* times to ensure there are no typos.

Do use proper grammar.

Don't send a letter more than one page long.

Don't write "enclosure;" obviously your resume is enclosed/attached.

# CHAPTER 5

# A Group Project

## NETWORKING ESSENTIALS

Whether it's getting a lead on a position or a potential networking contact or following up on a sent resume, having confidence and communication skills are key to making contact while on a job pursuit because making contact—personal contact—is essential to demonstrate your true ability.

After you send out a resume, unless it is made very clear there is to be no follow-up from candidates, a phone call or e-mail to confirm receipt is professional. It communicates attention to detail and follow-through.

Many people will tell you a phone call is better than an e-mail or vice versa. Do what comes natural to you. If you have already made contact or talked with the person, keep the personal connection by making a phone call. And if you are asking for something, then by all means pick up the phone to lend a personal touch to the request.

Verbal skills are crucial within the workplace environment, and making phone calls is another opportunity for you to show off your verbal prowess. Consider this part of the interview evaluation because you get to answer the question, "Can this person speak well?"

In addition to making contact to follow up on a sent resume, you also want to make contact to set up interviews—especially informational interviews to prepare you for the "real" thing by giving you impeccable interviewing skills and information about the field. Just as you need to know exactly what position you're interested in when going on an official interview, you need to know exactly what information you want to acquire when going on an informational interview. You don't want to be asked what position you seek and answer with "Anything you have available." Indecisiveness does not put forth a willing attitude—it just looks like a lack of focus. It's quite obvious that you can't go for what you want if you don't know what it is.

**ADVICE FROM THE CORNER OFFICE**
Samples of voicemails left for HR managers by graduates looking for jobs include: "Yeah, hey, this is Jordan, I sent in my resume. Why don't you go ahead and give me a call back, my number is . . . " and "Hi, um, this is Melonie, and, um, I, um, sent in my resume, and, um, am hoping you'll give me an interview?" So, should you choose personal contact via phone, practice your message ahead of time. And do know that many interviewers/recruiters won't call you back unless your qualifications match, but leaving an awkward voicemail could harm your chances should your resume have landed in the "yes" pile.

This chapter will focus on contacting people to set up informational interviews. Having these interviews provides insight (and practice) even if they don't lead to a position at a particular company. You can set up these types of meetings via networking or cold calling to find out what positions exist and what various careers actually entail. Create a list of potential companies, positions, and people with whom you'd like to meet. Don't go overboard here—think of this as research and stick to the specific avenues that will bring you the most information.

It is best to call the individuals to request an informational interview. However, if you only have an address (e-mail or otherwise), you can send a letter to request a meeting. The letter should be short and concise and spell out in certain terms what you are requesting.

Either way, via phone or letter, you want to make it clear that you only want thirty minutes (max) of someone's time, that you're not asking for a job, and that you're contacting this person because you respect his or her advice. Clearly explain who you are (a recent graduate) and why you are interested in setting up a meeting.

If you send a letter (or leave a voicemail), indicate what time you will call back—and then stick to it. "George" shared a story about how, after sending a letter to indicate he would follow up at a specific time, he reached the secretary of the executive he was trying to meet. Imagine his surprise (and joy) when the secretary said the executive had received the letter and was unable to talk at this particular time but had mentioned George may call. George followed up and did exactly what he said he would. This is a perfect demonstration of the follow-up and attention to detail that will help you land an informational interview—and maybe the job of your dreams!

You want to treat the informational interview with as much professionalism as a real interview. Be sure to bring a copy of your resume, dress in interview attire, have a list of questions, and be prepared to answer questions as well. Again, as noted in Chapter 3, this is a time to gather information about the field, positions within the field, and industry practices. Most who meet with you will understand that you're looking for a point of reference within the field.

## BE INNOVATIVE

Finding professionals who you can hit up for an informational interview is easier than ever now that our society is connected through social media platforms. Networking sites like Facebook (*www.facebook.com*), Gather (*www.gather.com*), and LinkedIn (*www.linkedin.com*) can help you find exceptional candidates with whom you can consult. Since you've made it through college, you are probably very familiar with these sites and most likely have profiles of your own on at least one social networking site, but if you don't, they are super easy to use. Setting up a basic account is uncomplicated and, of course, free.

LinkedIn is a more professional platform designed for business people who want to make connections. Once on the site, locate the "Groups" section and choose from hundreds of groups in your field of interest to join. Once part of the group, you can e-mail other members to join your personal network or send e-mails introducing yourself and expressing your interests. LinkedIn members are generally more than willing to help, since the site is wired to facilitate connections between professionals and entrepreneurs. Also, those who have set up a profile are probably reaching out to others themselves.

## CLASS NOTES

John, 26

Graduating from a very small college in the Midwestern state of Michigan, John found his university didn't offer much in the way of postgraduate guidance. He had studied political science and communication and **wasn't sure what direction** he wanted his career to take, so he took a couple of odd jobs, such as at the deli and at a clock shop, while he figured things out.

He decided to pursue a graduate degree at a state school in Michigan and studied urban planning and policy. He also **took an internship** with the governor of Michigan, which he received after calling the governor's office to inquire about opportunities. After one semester, he found the program at the school to be too "simple and not challenging," so he decided to move to a bigger city and pursue a career. He is now a sales professional for a large company in Chicago. He found the job via a contact he made while interning at the governor's office.

"Network and take every opportunity," John says. "I drove seventy or eighty miles to the internship with the governor; I paid for the gas from my student loans. But I found it was worth it; I have a job today because of it."

His advice: Don't turn anything down if you personally enjoy doing it. **Use every experience that comes your way** to help you in your job search. Sometimes knowledge and experiences you don't even know you have will help you land a job.

Plus, LinkedIn now offers a useful discussion platform where groups can share an ongoing dialogue about shared interests, and most of them focus on careers. Once you pose a question, you may be blown away by the caliber of professionals who actually participate in providing an answer. You can ask for referrals or ask the prospective respondents to point you in the right direction. You'll usually have an abundance of replies because there are plenty of LinkedIn group members who love to offer tips and advice. You can also search for jobs on this site and it will indicate if someone within your own network, or a group to which you belong, knows either the person who posted the job or someone at the same company. You can request an introduction and network to wrangle an interview this way, too. This resource is a useful tool for any job seeker, and it would be more than worthwhile to join and explore.

Facebook, which is less about business and more about social contacts, can still be utilized to a job hunter's advantage. This brilliant community was initially designed for college students but has globally expanded and now consists of every age group and socioeconomic profile. Facebook also offers groups you can join, and discussions are encouraged among group members. Join the ones that fit your career ambitions and start picking those clever comembers' brains. If you can't find groups relevant to your interests, start your own. Once you have a personal Facebook profile, name your group something like "Future Engineers of America" (or whatever your career field happens to be) and invite people who are in the same job-search boat.

You can also post your aspirations on your profile page, asking friends and other connections to help you find experts in your subject of interest. Again, this is the beauty of the social media world. Everyone wants to make contact and get in on the conversation, so make use of it. However, if your Facebook page has pictures of the last party you attended, or anything sexually suggestive or inappropriate, either clean it up and have only a professional-looking profile *or* make sure your page is set to private for everyone except friends and don't utilize this platform during your job search. Having a potential employer or network contact stumble onto something that could be deemed unprofessional is the last thing you want to happen.

**ADVICE FROM THE CORNER OFFICE**
Julie Grass, HR professional and founder of the Momentum Group, recommends: "Remember, even though an informational interview is not intended to land you a specific job, it gives you a connection with someone in the field who may prove helpful later on. It gives you an opportunity to get *real* perspective on the position/industry you are considering."

Gather is another site you might want to explore, though this is one of the more casual groups. There are hundreds of others, and more are launching constantly. Spend time searching the Internet to find social networking groups and peer networks to suit your needs and professional interests. The best place to start is on your college website, in the alumni section. Most schools and universities are implementing their own social sites and communities and proactively helping graduates find employment and success once out in the working world. The alumni office of your alma mater is one of the most resource-rich destinations from which you can draw information and specific direction. This department is entirely set up to support the goals of its graduates.

# CLASS NOTES

David, 28

Immediately after college, David found a job in the investment banking field through the career center on campus. **His approach was calculated**; he researched the companies he wanted to work for, uncovered the names and contact information of the hiring managers, and began a mailing blitz. He sent out fifty-five packets that included a cover letter, resume, letter of references, and a statement about what he did as an intern. He followed up his mailing with phone calls and was able to secure numerous interviews from which he received two job offers.

"I believe in the 'knock the door down' method so I tried to be **as persistent as possible** without being pushy, which is a tough balance," he says.

David's first position was in the mergers and acquisitions department, and his job was to work with owners of small companies to understand their industry and specific business model and thus provide valuation services for their potential sale. With the information he gathered, he put together a "pitch book" about each business to be shown to prospective buyers. He was with this company two years and **learned a great deal** about buying and selling businesses and properties.

From there he was hired by a commercial real estate investment brokerage firm where he started out in sales and now is a senior agent specializing in commercial shopping centers. He also oversees a team of other junior agents.

"I have mastered the art of the team player," David says. "And I think this characteristic was apparent when I talked with prospective employers; nowadays everyone's smart, you just have to rise above the other applicants!" He believes the most valuable assets on a job hunt venture are **motivation, drive, and the ability to demonstrate you can do the job**, do it right, and do it better than anyone else.

David is now involved with the USC undergraduate business school, his alma mater, where he mentors aspiring professionals. His advice to young job seekers: "**Find out who the players are in the industry** you want to work in and contact them directly. Don't get lost in someone's inbox—make the effort to make personal contacts."

If you are particularly creative, you can post a YouTube video, presenting yourself as a recent graduate investigating employment options. Be sure to ask for something—people won't know what you want unless you ask. Being the imaginative type, you can say you're looking for professionals in your field who are willing to give you thirty minutes for an informational interview. If you treasure your privacy, this won't work for you because you'll have to give some sort of contact information such as an e-mail address, and you may be stunned at how fast a video will make its rounds. A word of advice here: set up a separate e-mail box just for this endeavor. You won't want to swarm your personal account with the spam you'll unfortunately gather along with the legitimate responses. (Once you get your job, you can eventually delete this temporary account.)

You can also start a blog and work on linking with others of the same interests. Blogging has an amazing power to draw remarks and advice. Readers want to join in the conversation, and even the know-it-alls can contribute helpful tips. Blogs are easy to set up through services like blogspot (*www.blogger.com*) and TypePad (*www.typepad.com*).

If you want to target specific professionals, you can locate them by checking out posted podcasts on the web. Check out sites like podcast411 (*www.podcast411.com*), PodcastDirectory (www.*podcastdirectory.com*), or podscope (*www.podscope.com*). If you find a professional who impresses you, get her contact info and tell her you were motivated by her presentation and you'd like to spend less than thirty minutes interviewing her about her work. You'll find that many will be flattered and delighted to help out.

If you want to keep less exposed and simply send your info to people you trust, create a CD or a DVD stating your needs and mail it to specific professionals or others who can help you make connections. You'll gain attention and stand out as smart and innovative. Remember to keep it short, concise, professional, and designed to keep attention while asking for what you want. Try to come up with other off-the-wall, innovative ways to grab the attention of people who can help you. More than any other generation on the planet today, you know the value of the electronic world and you should make use of it when you're looking for people to consult with about your future work.

Explore every avenue available, including good old-fashioned word of mouth. With such concentrated effort, you're sure to make some phenomenal contacts who will help guide you to the job you want.

## SAMPLE PHONE SCRIPT: REQUESTING AN INFORMATIONAL INTERVIEW

*This is to call someone via a networking or mutual acquaintance lead:*

Hello {insert Mr. or Ms. Last Name}, my name is _____. I was talking with {insert name} whom I met through {insert organization, friend's name, or where you met*} and I mentioned that I wanted to learn how to break into the field of {insert field}. She/He said you went to college together and that you may be able to give me a few pieces of valuable advice as I look to learn more about this field. Would you be able to spare no more than thirty minutes for an informational interview so I could ask you some questions? I'm not asking for a job, just for some advice.

*This is to cold-call someone:*

Hello {insert Mr. or Ms. Last Name}, my name is _____. I am looking to learn more about {insert field}, and I know you are very successful within this field*. Would you be able to spare no more than thirty minutes for an informational interview so I could ask you some questions? I'm not asking for a job, just for some advice.

*You can also indicate how else you know about this person's success: Did she speak in your class? Did you see him on television? Have you read an article that quoted something he or she says?*

## SAMPLE LETTER:
## REQUESTING AN INFORMATIONAL INTERVIEW

*This is to write someone via a networking or mutual acquaintance lead:*

Dear {insert Mr. or Ms. Last Name},

I recently graduated {or state your present circumstances, such as "I am in my senior year as a business major at Penn State . . . ," or "I recently relocated to the Northeast . . ."} and am interested in a career in {insert field}. {Insert mutual contact name} suggested I contact you because you might have some great suggestions about breaking into this field. I'm not asking for a job, I'm just interested in researching as much as I can about this career path and what it takes to be successful.

I can be reached at {insert contact information}. I will also give you a call on Thursday at 3 P.M. EST to confirm if you'd be willing to meet or talk via phone. Thank you in advance.

Warmly,

{your full name}

*This is to write someone without a mutual contact:*

Dear {insert Mr. or Ms. Last Name},
I recently graduated {or whatever your circumstances} and am interested in a career in {insert field}. After much research, I have found it would be quite valuable to talk with you about breaking into this field. I'm not asking for a job, I'm just interested in learning as much as I can about this career and what it takes to be successful.
I can be reached at {insert contact information}. I will also give you a call on Thursday at 3 P.M. EST to confirm if you'd be willing to meet or talk via phone. Thank you in advance.
Warmly,
{your full name}

Communicate professional confidence at all times, know what you want, and go after it. Making contact and establishing relationships will not only help you figure out what you want but will help you get to where you want to be. ■

## cheat sheet

Don't miss a scheduled time to call if you said you'd call.

Don't be indecisive; it doesn't exemplify a "willing" attitude.

Do realize that people want to give you information—because they do!

Don't think informational interviews are a waste; you make great contacts.

Do be sure to follow up with any information gleamed from the contact.

## CHAPTER 6

# The Gift of Gab

## HANDLING A TELEPHONE INTERVIEW

> "Control your own destiny or someone else will."
>
> JACK WELCH

So you've sent your resume and the company is interested in bringing you in for an interview. Initially, many recruiters will conduct a telephone interview, as it is a good screening process. Sometimes they need to determine if you are, in fact, qualified before they bring you into the office to interview with senior managers. But phone interviews can be challenging, particularly if you have not participated in this type of a meeting before. You will need to think quick, provide applicable but concise answers, and convey a professional and enthusiastic demeanor. The conversation can last anywhere from fifteen to forty-five minutes, and the questions may be very specific or very general. Either way, this is your first chance to make a great impression, and you need to know how to make the best use of the opportunity.

## BE PREPARED

There are three primary types of telephone interviews:

1. A call at a preset date and time.
2. An unexpected call in response to your job application.
3. An impromptu phone interview that occurs on the spot when you call to inquire about a job opening.

In each of these cases, you need to be armed and ready to make a good impression. If you're sending out your resume and pursuing job options, it's important to be prepared for a potential phone interview. A hiring professional can call you at any time and ask if you have a few minutes to talk. Sometimes he might call to set up a time to talk at a later time, but stay on guard in case he wants to chat while he has you on the phone.

If for some reason it's not convenient for you to interview right on the spot, be cautious about how you will relay this information. Never say, "It's not a good time for me to talk right now, can you call back?" Instead, indicate your enthusiasm and rephrase your regret like this: "I'm thrilled to hear from you! I can spend a few minutes on the phone before I have to take off, will this be enough time or would you rather schedule another time where I can spend more time with you?"

When interviewed over the phone, you're essentially being screened to determine whether you are qualified for the position. (Even your phone etiquette counts, since you're likely to use the phone in some capacity at your new job.) The phone interview is the step that usually follows the resume submission and precedes an "in-person" interview. During the conversation, interviewers can initially verify if you're as capable as you sound on paper and if you're a good fit for the company.

Therefore, you should prepare for a phone interview just as you would for a face-to-face interview. Keep a copy of your resume in front of you so you can refer to specific details when asked (and you will be). You will most likely be queried about your skills, accomplishments, and professional or academic background. You will also likely be questioned about your strengths and how you plan to apply those to your desired position.

Lists help you stay on course and provide quick reference in case you feel caught off guard or get nervous. It is advisable to have a list of potential interview questions handy (more on this in Chapter 12) so you can quickly refresh your memory and not feel stumped.

**ADVICE FROM THE CORNER OFFICE**
**Michelle Poxson, an HR executive, says a phone interview is all about:**

- Your resume and walking the potential employer through your employment history/college classes and reasons you made certain choices to date.
- Making sure you meet the requirements for the job. Quickly highlight significant results achieved in course work, employment, and volunteering. Companies want talent that can speak results. This is really important.
- The ability to show that you can think on your feet, while giving them a sense of your personality.

Be sure to take notes while on the phone. Sometimes the interviewer will give hints about the company or the job that will help equip you for the in-person interview, and you can jot down questions you may have for the hiring manager or note anything that you may have to tend to after the call is complete. During the interview, you may realize that you are missing important information. Without a pen and paper handy, you may forget these details in the excitement of the moment.

**ADVICE FROM THE CORNER OFFICE**
**Nichole Addario DiModica, former vice president of operations and human resources for Dualstar Entertainment Group, gives this insight:**

- **I look for confidence in your voice; possibly even more confidence than you would exert in an in-person interview since I can't see you.**
- **Most often, I will know from a phone conversation if a person is right for a job and move on to an in-person interview as a second step. Phone interviews are a great time saver.**
- **If you're qualified, tell me how and why you became qualified to do the job. If you're just out of college and don't have a ton of experience, use the resources you do have. For example, if you were raised in an environment of family businesses, you have been exposed to different scenarios.**

Your objective is to solidify your candidacy. Provide details to support your resume, outlining your outstanding performance. Be sure to use numbers and facts as concrete figures; this is always effective. Be prepared to give specific details, and learn to summarize your professional experience in about a two-minute window.

When asked a question, avoid answering with a simple yes or no. Remember, this is your time to convince the hiring manager to bring you in for an interview. Use the opportunity to elaborate about your skills and qualifications. You may also be asked if you have questions prior to concluding the call, so be creative and ask about the company in a way that makes the recruiter feel you are genuinely interested in the job. Don't forget, an interview is nothing more than a sales pitch—you're trying to sell yourself to someone who has the authority to give you a job or call you in for a face-to-face interview.

Take a minute to write a quick thank-you note after the call. You want to take measures to single yourself out above the rest, and most applicants may not think to do this for a phone interview. Therefore, as soon as a potential interviewer calls, train yourself to pay attention to the person's name. You can always call the company's main line and ask the receptionist for proper spelling.

Here's a sample note:

"Thank you for taking the time to speak with me on the phone today about the sales position. I feel I understand more about your company and the position for which I've applied. I would love to schedule a personal interview with you to further discuss my qualifications for the job. I look forward to hearing from you."

## PHONE INTERVIEW PROS AND CONS

Interviewing by phone offers both advantages and disadvantages versus face-to-face interviewing. If you're prone to being nervous, a phone interview will be valuable to you. You can make use of notes to help you work through the questions you'll be asked. You can also focus entirely on your delivery, since you don't have to give much attention to your body language or appearance at the moment.

On the other hand, you aren't privy to the nonverbal cues that can help you through an in-person interview. When face to face with an interviewer, you can determine whether she seems interested, wants more detail, is impressed, or is ready to wrap it up by her physical language. Over the phone, you don't have this advantage.

Despite these disadvantages, a phone discussion can be to your benefit if you do a satisfactory job and land that personal interview.

**ADVICE FROM THE CORNER OFFICE**
**Sara Van Wagoner, senior executive, says she looks for the basics:**

- **Does he seem serious about looking for a job?**
- **How is her grammar?**
- **Can he think quickly and provide appropriate answers?**
- **What type of job/company does she want?**
- **What salary expectations does he have?**

## SAMPLE INTERVIEW QUESTIONS

Spend time rehearsing what you will say so you can be prepared to answer with confidence. Here are basic questions usually asked during a phone interview (you may also be asked these same questions during the face-to-face interview. Even more detailed answers are given in Chapter 12 for that scenario.):

1. Tell me about yourself.
   *No need to discuss your childhood here, just give a brief explanation about your general experience and your professional aspirations.*

2. What attracts you to our company?
   *Be ready for this one. Without getting too detailed, show that you know what they do and perhaps are knowledgeable about their products. (This also means that when you initially send out resumes, you should be aware of the background of each company.)*

3. What can you offer us that other applicants can't?
   *Describe specific details about ways you were able to solve problems with previous employers or in other endeavors under your supervision.*

4. What are you looking to gain from this job?
   *Explain how you plan to utilize your skills, develop further skills, and contribute what you know to benefit company goals. Avoid vague answers such as "I like working with people" and be specific with your reply: "I want to apply my mathematical skills to offer solutions to IT problems or situations at your company."*

5. Why do you want to leave your current job?
   *If you're fresh out of college, say so. But if you already have a job and want to move on, stay positive about your desire to grow and use more of your untapped skills. NEVER badmouth a company you worked for or a current or previous employer.*

6. Why should we hire you?
   *Be positive and enthusiastic. Here's a chance to elaborate on your strengths and how they can be of value to the company where you hope to work.*

Let the interviewer finish asking a question before jumping in with an answer. Carefully consider what has been asked before spewing out the first thing that comes to mind. If you didn't hear or didn't understand the question, it's quite acceptable to politely ask the interviewer to repeat or rephrase it. If you answer too quickly or don't listen carefully to what you're being asked, you may give the wrong response. Take your time and be as professional as possible.

Avoid fillers such as "uh," "um," "er," or "you know." These conversation don'ts are somehow amplified when they're spoken on the phone (more on this in Chapter 7). Also avoid slang such as "wanna" or "gonna"—you've worked hard for your college degree and certainly want to give off the impression of being well educated and well versed. Also, it seems silly to mention an obvious detail, but watch your language and don't use cuss words or vulgarities. Some people swear frequently during the course of normal conversation, and it can simply pop out of your mouth if you're not cognizant of it (and it has happened).

Be aware of the pace of your speech; speak slowly and clearly. If you talk too fast you may run out of breath or begin to sound nervous. However, if you speak too slowly you may sound monotonous or boring. Keep your voice upbeat and positive.

Feel free to break the starkness of the interview with occasional questions. You will want to know if it is worth your time to schlep into their office to interview with them. (Hint: it is always worth it for the interview experience, but you should go in with realistic expectations, too.) Ask the interviewer to tell you what the expectations are for this position and what the short- and long-term goals are for the company. This will establish you as an engaged applicant right from the get-go and may help to create a more relaxed conversation. Even if you are nervous, try to come across as confident. Keep in mind that most candidates are nervous at an interview, so it's perfectly understandable.

A phone interview will be short, but it's worth noting that though it may be tempting to embellish your accomplishments, don't! Be as honest with your answers as you can, and if you feel you fall short somehow, turn it around to your advantage: "I was at my previous position for nine months, but I'm hoping to find a job where I can devote myself and contribute." (Of course, this goes for the face-to-face interview, too!)

Be prepared to be specific. Your interviewer might ask a tough question that requires details about specific actions you might have personally taken to solve a problem or complete an assignment. He may pose the question so you can identify how you personally contributed, instead of talking about how you were part of the group working on a project. Using the word "I" rather than "we" will inform the interviewer of the important role you played as part of the achievement.

Once the interview is complete, ask the interviewer if you have answered all of his questions. Restate your interest in the job and ask what the next steps might entail.

## PHONE POSTURE

Everyone has a preferred phone stance. Some like to sit; others like to pace as they speak. The notion of telephone attitude is significant: Did you know your smile comes through your voice as you speak and that people tend to sound more confident when they're standing up during a phone conversation? This is because you project better and sound more certain of yourself. You must feel comfortable and self-assured in order to perform well. If you have an early morning call scheduled, you may want to shower and put on business attire to help you project confidence—even if it would be easier to take the call in your pajamas. However, if you feel confident sitting on the floor or in your pajamas, that's great! Since the caller can't see you, do whatever you have to do for added empowerment. Just be sure that you come across as secure, enthusiastic, and well spoken.

## YOUR OUTGOING MESSAGE

Now that you're a job applicant, you want to be as professional as possible in anything that will help you land a job. This applies to your phone habits as well.

**ADVICE FROM THE CORNER OFFICE**
Sara Van Wagoner, senior executive, offers an important tip: "Do not have singing, songs, or children on your voicemail. The interviewer will call her coworkers into her office to hear how ridiculous, annoying, or offensive the message is. But she will not leave a message or call you again. "

When recording a professional voicemail greeting, you'll first need to identify yourself so the caller is sure she has the correct number. If you're leaving a home number but live with roommates or numerous siblings who may not give you your phone messages in a timely fashion, consider investing in your own phone line, or give your cell phone number to interviewers.

It's important to return a call as soon as you can; however, if you get voicemail on the call back, you can leave a message, just be sure to leave your first and last name and the position you've applied for. This is especially important if you're returning a call from someone in human resources, as they tend to call applicants all day long. ■

## cheat sheet

Don't put the interviewer on hold while you answer call waiting.

Don't have music or the TV blasting in the background.

Don't chew gum or eat.

Do keep your answers short and concise.

Don't interrupt.

Do keep a record of where you've applied so you are prepared when you get a call.

Do keep your phone charged so the call is not dropped.

Do have a professional voicemail message.

Don't ask how much you'll get paid—you haven't been offered the job yet.

## CHAPTER 7

# Responsible Rhetoric

## WHAT YOU SHOULD AND SHOULDN'T SAY

> "Words mean more than what is set down on paper. It takes the human voice to infuse them with shades of deeper meaning."
>
> MAYA ANGELOU

Fillers ("like" and "um"), qualifiers ("Do you know what I mean?" and "Does this make sense?"), along with speaking in uptalk (ending every sentence as a question) will diminish your credibility. These communication blunders impede your ability to be taken seriously. They also make you sound young and uneducated. And while you may be a new grad, you're anything but uneducated.

If you listen to any executive or well-known person, you don't hear qualifiers, uptalk, or clichés. Why? Because they don't project confidence or leadership. When interviewing, you not only want to be taken seriously as a contributor or a leader but also as a reliable contact who is capable of working with clients. Clients want to feel their accounts, products, and businesses are in the hands of someone who can handle it. Perception is reality in this instance. Whether you can or can't handle the potential job may not be the issue; it will come down to *if* they *think* you can—and a lot of this will come from how you demonstrate your communicative abilities. Remember, monitoring these blunders demonstrates instant professionalism.

So while some of this may seem troublesome, review your skills with the tools outlined in this chapter just to be sure you don't unknowingly fall into one of these categories.

## THE UPTALK OF IT

The sky is blue? The grass is green? I am smart? Why the question marks? It's called uptalk! Listen and you'll hear it. It's the speech pattern where people say an affirmative sentence but make it sound like a question with the rising inflection at the end of a sentence. This has become the speech epidemic of our time.

If you have lunch with friends or visit with family, it's there. You may even be guilty too! Where did uptalk come from? Some say it originated in the San Fernando Valley with teenagers and the Valley Girl craze. But it's now heard across genders and generations, in colleges, boardrooms, and throughout the country. Characters on television shows speak with uptalk, and *South Park* even highlighted the speech in an episode.

Experts say this type of speech is used because speakers feel uptalk softens speech. People don't feel as though they are lecturing others but are instead engaging them in conversation and asking for input.

But uptalk—you'll catch it if you listen closely—implies youthfulness, insecurity, and uncertainty. Using uptalk can make you come across as unprofessional and longing for acceptance.

Imagine you're in a meeting and introduce yourself as, "Hi, my name is Jennifer? And we're going to look at our sales growth? Welcome to all of you?" Won't everyone be thinking: Are you sure your name is Jennifer? Are you sure we're looking at sales growth? Are you sure you're welcoming me?

It can also completely throw off your interview, too. "Hi, my name is John? It's nice to meet you? . . .

This constant talking in questions can, for a split second, be somewhat amusing. Yet implying uncertainty isn't entertaining to employers or interviewers who want the people who are representing their business to exude confidence. Chances are, if you want to be chosen to be part of a project, or are asking for a job or raise, you won't get it. People want people who exude confidence.

So ask your friends and family to tell you if they catch you using uptalk. Work to realign your speech to be affirmative, to say sentences with strength, and to portray yourself as able and confident. Who knows, maybe you'll even get the job you're after! Using these three basic steps will make a difference:

- Identify the use of uptalk.
- Practice saying affirmative sentences with an affirmative ending.
- Work with a partner(s) who is given carte blanche freedom to tap you, point at you, or even charge a dollar when they hear uptalk—not only will you improve your speech, you can buy the person lunch!

## LIKE, UH . . .

Sometimes it is hard to have a complete stream of thought if you're put on the spot or when nerves come into play. But when every other word is "uh," ah," "um," or "like,"—to name just a few of the filler words—you lose a piece of your wow factor; the confidence you're trying to demonstrate to your interviewer, boss, or anyone listening to you is lost. They are too distracted to properly assess your qualifications.

Filler words are common, but they can be overcome! This is not something you want in the professional environment, especially when making presentations, answering interview questions, or talking with a supervisor.

Let's look at the word "like." Everybody uses it. It is more common in certain parts of the country, but it is heard in most cities. In fact, when we asked professionals about this particular word, everyone overwhelmingly either started to laugh (because they recognize it as "a ridiculous part of the culture," as one person noted), or started nodding as though they understood it as a given part of young people's speech.

Lose the "like"! Just stop saying it. If you're guilty of it, know that it makes you sound young and uneducated. There's just no other way to put it. And if you think you don't do it, make sure! Ask someone or stick a tape recorder on the table at lunch and record a conversation.

The trick to losing the "likes," the "uhs," and the "ums" is to be really conscious of your speech. Once in a class, during a twelve-minute presentation, we counted thirty-two "ums" uttered as a filler words by an educated graduate student. *Painful.* Many people in the class were snickering, yet no one bothered to tell the presenter. But then again, how do you tell someone how painful it was to listen to a presentation she just gave?

If your "likes" and "ums" are, like, really bad, speech-language pathologist Lynn Esser suggests specific activities to minimize your usage. Steps include working with a partner and using a buzzer or chips to monitor the fillers during conversations. The other person will hold a conversation with you and buzz every time you say "like," so you are aware of how often. You can also ask someone with whom you spend a great deal of time to ask for $1 every time you say it. After several dollars, you'll be conscious! And you can then donate the money.

If you're really conscious of your speech, speak slowly, and are aware of every word you say, you can break the habit of using filler words. Losing the question-like inflection at the end of sentences, and the "likes" and "ums," instantly propels you to a professional speaking level. You will be taken seriously in the business world. Stopping may also simply be a matter of becoming comfortable with who you are and what you can say. If you're not comfortable, figure out how to become so. Once you're confident in what you're saying, the words will flow easier and sound better, too.

**ADVICE FROM THE CORNER OFFICE**
Speech-language pathologist Lynn Esser says if an interview or a formal public speaking arrangement is in sight, you should have a well-practiced script on the subject matter and should rehearse to make sure you're using an appropriate vocal tone, quality, inflection, and expressions/gestures.

## VOICE, TONE, AND PITCH, OH MY!

Vocal tone and pitch are essential to being taken seriously. Tone is the quality of speech; pitch is the frequency of vibration. A high-pitched, high-tonal voice is not only difficult to listen to for a long period of time, but it also casts a shadow on being taken seriously.

There's something to be said about one's voice quality (no pun, intended). It sets a mood (think NPR or smooth jazz announcers) or creates a wonderful persona (think Fran Drescher or the many character voices someone like Seth Green provides). Voice is important.

But in an interview, office, or boardroom, you definitely don't want to sound whiny, character-like, or similar to a radio announcer. Assess your voice quality. Women tend to have a higher-pitched voice (obviously), but sometimes it is too high! Add uptalk to a high-pitched voice, and it can be really difficult to listen. Find a digital recorder to capture the sound of your voice. How does it sound? You want to learn to control the tone and pitch of your voice.

**ADVICE FROM THE CORNER OFFICE**
**Speech-language pathologist Lynn Esser looks at improving voice quality: "You want to address decreasing vocal abuse, avoiding hoarseness of voice, determining optimal pitch, increasing clarity, projecting the voice, reducing nasal voice production, and avoiding a breathy voice quality. Ask yourself (or others for second and third opinions) if your voice is soft, hoarse, harsh, breathy, loud, tonic, and/or wet. Are the intonation patterns appropriate for the statement(s) made (exclamation, declaration, question, etc.). Begin with awareness. Use a mirror as a visual aid for help. Recording and/or videotaping are usually successful with voice quality and infliction."**

While guys have a lower voice, sometimes it comes across too monotone. Grab a digital recorder to listen to your own voice. Be sure to fluctuate your tone; there's nothing worse than a deep, low-toned, monotone drone. It puts interviewers to sleep—or at least out to daydream.

If you're thinking, "But this is my voice!," well, yes it is, but actors, people who migrate to this country, and professional speakers learn to tweak their voices all the time. It is possible. So while you may not need professional tweaks, you definitely want to make sure you sound professional.

Breathing via the diaphragm (stomach in and out) versus breathing via the chest (shoulders up and down) will ensure air is processed properly. But also really being conscious of one's own tone and pitch and how the voice sounds is also crucial.

In order to work on your voice, it is important to know some factors capable of influencing voice production. For example, smoking, alcohol, caffeine, and gastroesophageal reflux may promote laryngitis, as will screaming, yelling, and excessively loud laughing. Allergies may also impact voice quality and production. Sometimes there are physiological, neurological, or psychological problems interfering with accurate production patterns.

If there are true abnormalities in voice production, you can see a trained professional such as an otolaryngologist (an ear-nose-throat doctor), especially if there is a severe problem, or a speech-language pathologist. A trained professional doctor (ENT) can diagnose or rule out the possibility of a serious condition. To decrease vocal abuse:

- Avoid talking in noisy places.
- Don't shout or yell.
- Use an easy onset of speech, such as using words beginning with "h" (how, who, hay, high).

- Decrease use of alcohol, caffeine, spicy foods, and smoking.
- Drink plenty of water.
- Rest the voice when possible (stay quiet, but don't whisper . . . whispering may cause more damage).

## INCREASING VOICE CLARITY

A common problem many people encounter is decreased clarity of speech, sometimes referred to as mumbling. To increase your clarity of speech, slow down the rate of speech and focus on articulating the sounds in words correctly. Breath control exercises can also help improve clarity. Yawning can help relax the muscles used when speaking. Practicing in front of a mirror and attempting to lip read the sounds in words may also help to increase awareness.

And here's something you may not know: You may instinctively turn down your voice volume during an interview or a presentation. This is normal and happens to most people when they feel anxious or intimidated, particularly to those who tend to be on the shy side already.

You may have been taught to speak politely, softly, or courteously when you were growing up, and that works in some situations: church, funeral, wedding, library. But in the boardroom—you need to be heard.

Projecting your voice can be easily learned with practice. A small digital recording device can go a long way in helping you become a more accomplished speaker. Place the unit across the room as you practice speaking and work on raising your volume to a point where you sound natural yet professional.

As you play back your voice recording, you may note that you have trouble articulating certain words. Proper enunciation is vital in a communication exchange, and learning to pronounce words correctly can save you from a steady stream of hearing the embarrassing, "I'm sorry . . . can you repeat that again?" remarks.

Speaking aloud and enunciating well is a universally notable and appealing trait. In fact, it's so prized that people who are particularly articulate can make a lot of money as voice-over talent for radio and television work. You may have noticed that speakers who enunciate well speak slowly and with determination. Speaking clearly is one of the first characteristics an interviewer will detect when you first meet.

But even if you have trouble in the enunciation department, there are exercises you can practice in order to help you improve. For example, stand in front of the mirror and repeat words to help you loosen your mouth, tongue, and jaw. Make each sound distinct as you exaggerate both consonants and vowels. You can also revisit your childhood and repeat those annoying tongue twisters that use to drive your mom crazy during carpool. Believe it or not, those silly sayings are great vocal exercises. Even the simple act of reading out loud can train you to enunciate correctly and help make you more aware of speaking with clarity.

Some voice specialists recommend the use of a pencil inserted horizontally in your mouth while you speak, as it forces you to enunciate more efficiently. But, unless you want to feel like a goofball or risk accidental choking, with continued practice the other exercises should do the trick. Also, don't underestimate the power of standing or sitting straight. Proper posture will definitely enable you to project your voice.

### Projecting the Voice

Here are exercises used to help increase volume:

- Speak when you breathe out.
- Take slow, deep breaths of air, completely filling the lungs, and pushing the stomach area out. Let out the air and say "ahhhhh" in a loud voice.
- After taking a deep breath, let the air out and count for as long as you can in a loud voice on the single breath. You can also use a rote monologue, such as the Pledge of Allegiance, the alphabet, or cadence.
- Drinking water to keep hydrated and avoiding milk, juice, and soda (carbonation may weaken the voice) may also help.

### Talking Too Loud

On the other hand, there are those who talk too loud. Recruiters have noted that this is particularly apparent in those in their twenties. Many believe that this is a cultural thing, similar to the use of uptalk and "like." So, you may want to ask someone you really trust to give an honest critique of your voice quality. Do you speak too soft? Are you speaking too loud? Do you speak with clarity? These are all factors that will ultimately help your communication skills, and help you be taken a serious contender in the workplace.

## I QUALIFY

"Qualify" here doesn't mean your job qualifications; it's adding a tag line seeking approval at the end of your sentences. There's no need to say something and then follow it up with, "Does this make sense?" or "Do you know what I mean?" State what you want to say, and leave it alone.

Sometimes, perhaps when giving complicated directives, you'll want to confirm that your listener understands. But some people do it after every sentence, within every conversation. It's definitely not necessary and makes you sound as though you're a poor communicator because you have to confirm clarification(s) every time you speak.

Another form of qualifying is saying, "I could be wrong, but . . . " or "I'm not sure this is right, but . . . " Again, this negates your credibility in your listener's eyes. If you're confident in what you want to say, say it; don't qualify.

**ADVICE FROM THE CORNER OFFICE**
La'Trise Smith, assistant vice president of human resources at Huntington Bank, reminds you not to speak in slang: Using "like," "You know what I'm saying?," or "You feel me?" creates an atmosphere of being too casual, too comfortable. Keep up the professionalism at all times during the interview.

## AVOIDING CLICHÉS LIKE THE PLAGUE

A cliché is a trite expression, a figure of speech considered to be overused or unoriginal. Using clichés is a slippery slope. You may feel like the cream of the crop, but in reality, you're not really hitting anything out of the ballpark. See how the communicative phrases of clichés take away the ability to sound original and articulate?

## cheat sheet

**Do** know that filler words diminish credibility.

**Do** avoid speaking in clichés.

**Don't** state an affirmative sentence as if it sounds like a question (uptalk).

**Don't** qualify sentences in search of justification or approval.

**Do** enunciate your words clearly.

**Do** listen for tone and make sure you aren't too high pitched or too low and monotone.

**Do** project with confidence; don't speak too softly or too loudly.

**Don't** use slang in your interview or create a casual environment.

Used effectively, a cliché can embellish a statement—it can paint a familiar picture or underscore a point. But clichés mostly seem silly and contrite. So use them sparingly. Speaking in clichés is a technique commonly used by those who want to get a point across without saying much. So how can you express your thoughts? Go ahead and use the word "I"—own what you want to say. Do you want to present something to someone? Think about how can you articulate it in comparative terms without using a cliché. Instead of answering the question "Why did you decide to look for a new job?" with "It's a dog-eat-dog world out there and a man has to do what a man has to do," consider responding with "Everyone has to take charge of his own career, and I knew it was time to move on because that's what's best for me." Express yourself without the common cliché and really impress your interviewers with your intelligence and excellent communications skills.

Pay attention to how you speak, put forth a professional image, and make the most of your interviews. Remember, even the smallest details can make a world of difference. ∎

## CHAPTER 8

# What Not to Wear

## APPROPRIATE OFFICE ATTIRE

> "The rules of hair care are simple and finite. Any Cosmo girl would have known."
>
> **REESE WITHERSPOON**
>
> **As Elle Woods in** *Legally Blonde*

It would be much simpler if applicants were hired solely on professional skills and qualifications rather than on appearance. In reality, your attire will undoubtedly be evaluated at first glance. And in today's competitive business environment, every detail matters. This doesn't mean you have to invest in an Armani ensemble, but you should be sure your clothes are clean and wrinkle-free. If an interviewer can't get past your unbuttoned shirt, your flip-flops, or your dandruff, it can dilute your power to sell yourself.

The days of stuffy three-piece suits and conservative below-the-knee skirt sets are long gone (yay!). Today's professional works in a world where individuality is defined through attire. Even though our twenty-first-century business culture is now more casual than ever, you should still dress to fit the job you hope to get. If your interview is at a law office, you'll want to wear something more conservative, such as a suit. If you are applying for a job at a tattoo parlor, you can probably get by with jeans and a casual shirt. But if you show up at the law firm in jeans or at the tattoo salon in a suit, expect to be passed over for the position. Dress for the field in which you're applying, but always be professional.

**ADVICE FROM THE CORNER OFFICE**

Michelle Poxson, an HR executive, says: Being well-dressed is important when making a good first impression, and the interviewer should be focused on what you say, not distracted by what you are wearing. Here are some tips:

- Consider the environment of the company where you are interviewing, that is, conservative, fashion forward, or casual/innovative.
- After this, still lean toward the conservative side with a sharp, well-tailored suit and expressing style/creativity with accessories: great handbag, earrings, scarf, tie, shoes, cufflinks.
- If the dress code is business casual, take it down one notch from the traditional suit: men can wear a suit without a tie; women can wear a skirt with a nice blouse.
- Once you get hired, look around to see what other successful and credible employees wear. Follow their lead.

Remember, as superficial as it may be, appearances do matter and everyone makes judgments. Your attire sends a message about your work ethic, and prospective employers will think less of you if you don't dress appropriately. Dress to suit your personality, but keep within professional standards. Regardless of the dress code within a particular company, your best bet is to dress on the conservative side when you go for your interview. You can adapt to the specific office dress code once you actually get the job, but if you question the appropriateness of an outfit, it probably isn't right.

## GENDER-SPECIFIC WEAR

### Women

If you plan to wear a sleeveless top, don't forget to shave your underarms (this might be basic information, but you'd be surprised how often it goes unheeded!). But really, this is more about keeping Saturday night clothes separate from your work clothes. Your work clothes should not be see-through (not that your Saturday clothes are, but just in case), and also save the miniskirt, patterned hosiery, bare midriff, and low-cut top for the night out at the club.

If your business suit includes a skirt, you want to keep to a traditional hemline, about one to two inches above the knee, a length that flatters most women. Be stylish, but dress to enhance your professional image. If you're planning to wear a blouse to your interview, double-check to ensure it doesn't gap in the front. You don't want your interviewer to be distracted by what's beyond those buttons. And by all means wear a bra, but be sure the strap is not peeking out.

Attention to detail pertains to your makeup application, too. Smoky eye makeup can be glamorous for an evening out with friends, but it's out of place in a corporate setting. Footwear also plays a key part in your presentation: stilettos and open-toed shoes are more fitting for social events, so keep footwear in vogue but more business oriented—a nice, stylish, closed-toe shoe has professional appeal. People can tell a lot by a shoe; clean, unscuffed shoes cinch up the professionalism of an outfit.

Even nail polish is a consideration. Trimmed nails with a subtle polish color are simple and appropriate.

**ADVICE FROM THE CORNER OFFICE**
Sara Van Wagoner, senior executive, offers these tips to dress the part:

- It is ALWAYS appropriate to wear a suit to an interview.
- Buy a good quality black, navy, or brown suit, cut in a timeless style—you will use this forever!
- Wear good quality shoes. Very high heels or shoes you would wear to a wedding are not appropriate for interviewing.
- Even more important than the shoes and suit is the bag you carry (if you are a woman). The bag/purse you carry should be of very good quality and style—people DO look at these things. A great bag tells a lot about the person (as does a cheap and unattractive bag).
- There is one condition when standard code should be ignored: if the person setting up the interview tells you something different. For example, some organizations such as Harley Davidson DO NOT want people to wear suits because their culture does not support this type of dress.

This doesn't mean you have to be unstylish. Work-appropriate fashion is a huge part of professionalism, but be careful. You don't want your wardrobe to say, "Since I have limited skills and am basically inexperienced, I'm hoping I can get your attention with how I look." Remember, be stylish, not cute. Be savvy, not sexy. It makes a big difference in how you're perceived.

### Men

Some of you may have great fashion sense, others have been perfectly comfortable rolling out of bed and wearing the crumpled jeans and T-shirt on the floor to your early morning classes. Some of you may opt to wear baggy pants with your boxers showing, but boxers sneaking out of your pants don't present a professional image, so fold in your underwear before you meet your prospective boss. And, unless you're applying for a position with a hip-hop band, droopy pants are a big no-no. Guys often opt for comfort, but even if it is your favorite (or lucky) shirt that you want to wear under your suit jacket, restrain yourself and present a positive, professional impact.

When dressing for an interview, wear a suit that fits. If you need to buy a new one, invest. If you need to borrow, do so from someone the same size because how you look truly makes a statement. Some of you may enjoy dressing professionally; others may find it a pain. Unfortunately, it is part of the deal when interviewing. So tuck your shirt into your pants on each side, wear a tie and suit jacket, and present the best you possible.

Facial hair is a personal preference. Unless you have deliberate facial hair like a goatee or mustache, you definitely want to show up to your appointment with a clean-shaven face. Of course, nails should be filed down and clean. Shoes always make the detailed statement of class. Stylish footwear here means something appropriate, clean, and tear-free. And, of course, keep your trendy combat boots and athletic shoes at home. You also want to remember to wear a belt that matches your shoes ( black belt with black shoes). If you're wearing a tie, which is highly recommended, make sure it's not decorated with hula dancers or cartoon characters; keep it simple and conservative.

### Women and Men

Showing up to an interview with greasy or uncombed hair is viewed as a sure sign that you don't pay attention to hygiene. Remember, the employer is counting on the employees to be a positive reflection of the company, and your messy head of hair may announce you have a streak of disorderliness.

You may be thinking that you've been banned from wearing anything you own, so now what? Following is a list of the basics you'll want to have ready to wear to an interview.

## BUSINESS WEAR FOR INTERVIEWS

Don't give the interviewer an opportunity to rule you out simply because you didn't make the time to iron your shirt or polish your shoes. Plan ahead, even the night before, by setting aside what you'll wear and deciding on how you'll wear it. Here is a basic cheat sheet to help you out when you're ready to put yourself together and head out to that long-awaited interview:

### Women

- *Suits:* Choose suits with jackets and skirts to fit your body type. If you consider your lower body to be a problem area, wear a flattering long jacket to cover your hips. Wool is the best fabric choice, unless you're interviewing in Phoenix in mid-August. It lasts the longest and looks the most professional. For summer, cottons and linens are good choices. (Be wary of linen, though, because it does wrinkle.) Dark blue, black, taupe, charcoal, or white (in season) are all acceptable colors. It's most appropriate to wear dark colors in winter and light colors in the spring and summer. Avoid loud colors no matter the season.

- *Shirts:* Cotton, silk, or cashmere is always a good choice. Transparent fabric is always inappropriate. Be sure to coordinate your blouse color with your suit color.

- *Shoes:* Low-heeled pumps are most suitable for business situations. Heels can be as high as an inch and a half or two inches, but too much higher than this is considered unprofessional. Open-toed shoes, wedges, mules, or sandals are inappropriate for business meetings.

- *Belts:* Belts should be leather and match the colors of your outfit. Avoid plastic, fur, or loud metallic belts and those studded with designs or jewels.

- *Jewelry:* Select tasteful, traditional pieces, and keep away from anything that clangs or jingles.

- *Hair and nails:* Your hair should be styled neatly (preferably just one color), and you should have manicured nails and light makeup. Also, go easy on the perfume.

- *Extras:* Bring a portfolio or briefcase containing extra copies of your resume and any other samples you may need to present.

**Men**

- *Double-breasted suits:* Not frequently worn today, but if you get your hands on a designer piece, always keep the jacket entirely buttoned.

- *Single-breasted suits:* The classic conservative suit colors are navy blue, gray, and charcoal. When standing, all buttons except for the bottom one are fastened. In fact, you never need to fasten the bottom button of a single-breasted suit jacket. To prevent bunching, a single-breasted jacket should be completely unbuttoned while you are seated.
- *Shirts:* The classic conservative shirt colors are light blue and white. All buttons of the shirt, including the top one, should be buttoned. Be sure the color of your suit and the shirt complement each other.
- *Ties:* Neckties should be darker than your shirt. They should be a solid color or may have a small conservative print. The bottom of the tie should touch or just go over the top of the belt buckle.
- *Belts and shoes:* These should be brown or black, preferably leather, and they should match one another. Shoes should not have rubber soles.
- *Socks:* Socks should match the pant leg. If that's not possible they can match your shoes.
- *Hair and nails:* Your hair should be trimmed, and your hands and nails should be clean.
- *Extras:* Bring a portfolio or briefcase containing extra copies of your resume and any other samples you may need to present.

Be sure to select comfortable, well-fitting clothes. You don't want to constantly be fiddling with a bow that keeps getting untied or a pair of pants that keep riding up. If your clothes are itchy, wear something else. You don't want to look irritated as you try to concentrate on your interview.

And remember, you don't need to spend a ton of money to have style. Invest in a few classic pieces that will likely last for years and cut corners by not purchasing too many trendy fashions that may fade fast. You may want a few pieces to modernize your attire (a professional but trendy blouse, for example). But overall, classic pieces like simple black pumps, a black or navy pant or skirt-suit, and a white blouse for women, and a dark suit, crisp long-sleeve shirt, solid colored tie, and conservative shoes for men should be your starting point. If you invest in quality pieces, you'll get a lot of use out of them throughout the years. Whatever you finally choose to wear, just be sure your clothing isn't frayed, your outfit is wrinkle free, and your footwear is not scuffed.

## COMPANY DRESS CODE

Once you get the job, you must continue to dress professionally (based on the expectations of the organization). It will help you to continue to build credibility.

**ADVICE FROM THE CORNER OFFICE**
Sara Van Wagoner, senior executive, says: "Business casual is well-pressed slacks and either a button-up shirt or blouse; a properly fitted sweater vest is also appropriate. Again, the shoes should be good quality and in good condition. Men—always wear socks—there is never a time when it is appropriate to wear shoes without socks to work."

Companies are now widely instituting a casual or business casual policy, sometimes once a week (casual Fridays), once a month, or on an ongoing basis. Many organizations have found that a relaxed dress code boosts employee morale and seems to increase productivity, which makes for a higher quality work environment.

But it's important to understand what casual or business casual really means to your employer before you come up with your own interpretation. If you assume a dress code by looking at the way the other employees were dressed on the day of your interview, you could make a big mistake. There may have been a special event or a dress-down day at the time. Because these terms have different definitions from one employer to another, no one will be able clarify this better than the human resources professional at your new place of employment—so ask!

### Business Casual

In general, business casual consists of the following choices:

WOMEN
- A more casual cotton or wool pant, or a conservative A-line skirt
- Sweaters or knit tops
- Open-toed sandals or wedges

MEN
- Khakis or cotton pants
- Short-sleeved shirts, polo shirts, or sweaters
- Ties optional

Sometimes, if your workplace has a casual dress code or a casual day, jeans are appropriate to wear. With so many options in terms of styles, colors, and price points, denim is comfortable for most people. However, before you saunter into work in your best jeans, be sure to ask if denim is acceptable at your workplace. Even if jeans are permitted, never wear jeans that are stained, torn anywhere, or frayed at the seams. Choose a dressier jean to wear on casual denim days.

### Read the Code

Management configures its dress code to reflect a professional and orderly organization. Read this policy carefully and follow it explicitly since your supervisor will likely enforce it. You may be asked to go home and change if you are not dressed to code, and if you are a repeat offender, it can ultimately cost you your job. ∎

## cheat sheet

Don't wear clothing with foul language or sexually suggestive or obscene images.

Do wear clean, classic, and comfortable professional attire.

Do keep business casual wear on the conservative side.

Do ask human resources for clarification on the dress code as needed.

Don't wear flip-flops or scuffed or old shoes.

Don't wear evening or party wear, workout clothes, or sweat suits.

Don't wear baseball caps or any kind of hat.

Do tuck in your underwear: boxers, bra straps.

## CHAPTER 9

# The Candid Candidate

## MASTERING THE ART OF SMALL TALK

Street slang, and casual words are cool to use with friends and trendy in certain settings; however, in the workplace, you need to use power words. To hear an articulate speaker is like listening to great music. Powerful words convey powerful messages. And as you enter the professional realm, words will help you get what you want out of life.

In an age where e-mail (or even texting) is the preferred mode of communication, verbal conversation has taken a back seat to the Internet when it comes to relaying information. And why not? E-mail offers absolute convenience (you can send a message when you feel like it; your recipients can respond when they feel like it). Plus you don't actually have to speak with anyone and suffer through stories about their kids or last night's bad date.

But no matter how popular the Internet continues to be, you'll never get away from actually having to speak with a live human. Whether you're trying to make a deal, get an answer, or provoke an action, getting to your point quickly and succinctly will always work in your favor. Learning to speak effectively and with brevity will help your listener understand what you need and help you get it.

Speaking well is an art form. Some are better at it than others, but everyone can learn to use professional words to inspire actions. Consider the power in the following statement:

"The position that just opened in the marketing department appeals to me because I can utilize my skills more effectively and contribute more to the company. I'd like to apply for the job."

It articulates why you want the job without hemming or hawing. It uses powerful, concise words.

Eliminating slang and using terms such as "I will," instead of "I can try," or "During the course of my research I uncovered" instead of, "I think I can remember" can announce your competency and single you out as a go-getting power speaker.

During your college years you learned to develop a speaking style appropriate for talking with peers or meeting someone for a date. This conversational approach was no doubt casual and sprinkled with lingo that was understood by your friends and may or may not have made sense to other people. But when you move from social circles into professional arenas, your speech will have to sound more proficient and less figurative, and you'll want to come across as clear and understandable as possible. Words are tools in your impression-making line of attack, and the more capable you sound to your prospective employer, the better chance you have of nailing the job you're after.

You use language to get what you want and to express how you feel. But you may not always be aware of the power of your words on those with whom you speak. As the old adage goes, words can heal or destroy. Words can also get you hired or disqualify you from a position. A simple statement can bear amazing results or can sabotage a career in the blink of an eye. Understanding how to use spoken language to your advantage includes being knowledgeable in everything from power verbs to appropriate casual conversation to being articulate and concise when you need to be.

## POWER VERBS

You were advised to start every sentence with a power or action verb when writing a resume. Carry this advice over into your speaking abilities, too. When you think about answering questions during an interview, contributing on a project at work, or addressing a conflict in the workplace, think in terms of power verbs: you *maximized,* you *created,* you *led,* you are *determined,* profits have *increased.*

Fill your vocabulary with powerful words. Make a list of your favorite verbs, then memorize them and use them often so they become a natural part of your speaking ability. Here are some examples of how to use action/power verbs in sentences:

I *created* a program for the student government to run more efficiently.

I *aced* an impromptu project the professor assigned.

I *facilitated* new student orientation seminars every fall and spring.

I *proved* it to be true by committing myself to the cause.

I *determined* how the problem should be solved after much deliberation and commitment.

I *led* the student body to petition for a vote that won by a landslide.

It was my idea that *funded* the sorority or fraternity project to completion.

## ADVICE FROM THE CORNER OFFICE

Susan Sellani-Hosage, a senior manager in human resources, says: "When I have the opportunity to speak to students about interviewing, I tell them it's like a verbal test and you're the subject. Make sure you select high-impact adjectives to describe yourself. Your words create the visual picture of the employee you will be at work. No one will hire someone who's 'pretty good' when they can hire someone who's 'conscientious, proficient, and

## A CAN-DO ATTITUDE

In a professional environment, affirmative words can take you far. The power verbs previously mentioned, along with the phrases "I'll take that on," "let me attempt to solve this," or "this is my plan" can be so valuable to an employer. Strong, positive words demonstrate that an employee is eager and motivated—qualities that will propel one forward in a corporate environment. On the other hand, complaining about a workload or blaming others for mistakes can have a stifling effect on a career because they reflect an employee's pessimistic attitude.

Capable and energetic people are natural magnets because of their contagious enthusiasm. They generally use affirmative phrases to express their level of confidence and vigor, and to inspire confidence and vigor in others: "I'm doing great, how are you?" "That's fabulous!" and "Great to see you!" These are simple phrases, but they are used enthusiastically by the upbeat bunch. After all, who doesn't want to be around a person who's positive and makes them feel good about themselves?

Conversely, negative people seem to have the opposite effect: Who wants to be around those who whine or nitpick? "I'm not so well today," "I hate my job," or "I'm so tired" are terms that the downers often say.

Given the choice, most people want to be with—and interviewers want to hire—cheerful, optimistic people who speak words that energize and encourage.

## GET TO THE POINT AND BE READY

Requesting a raise or a job, sealing a deal, or interacting with an interviewer are all cases where you need to avoid rambling and ask for what you want in an organized and efficient manner. Practice your phrases; practice your words. Not only is the choice of words important, but how they are delivered is of utmost importance, too.

This may sound complicated, but it's simple. All you need is a paper and pen, or laptop, handy. Jotting the following information down will enable you to organize your thoughts, which will lead to a skillful delivery. Plus, it will help you avoid the common "um" and "uh" that make their way into most conversations or voicemail messages.

First, know your objective. Second, know the request you want to make. As a personal exercise, ask yourself to encapsulate what you actually want in one sentence. Pretend you want an appointment with a marketing manager so you can get a job with the department. She is likely inundated with requests, so your appeal will have to be compelling from the get-go. Your condensed wish is to get an appointment, so jot this down.

*Objective:* "I want to be hired by Ms. B at XYZ company."
*Request:* "I would like to schedule an appointment to see Ms. B."

Now identify three reasons why you believe this person will benefit by meeting with you. When you have clarified those, place each reason in categories A, B, and C in the order of importance.

A. I am skilled and trained for this position.
B. My knowledge will help Ms. B's department achieve its marketing targets.
C. Ms. B is busy but needs to hire the best person for the job, and I can present my pitch quickly and with competence.

Once this is established, be sure to know why you are skilled and trained for this position. Maybe you did an internship with a leading marketing firm and were able to sit in on many product development discussions. You were part of the team of a major product launch at the company where you interned.

By now you should be able to easily come up with the final and most important point of your message: what you actually need from your contact. In this case it's for Ms. B to give you the job. You need to realize and break down your objectives, support the reasons behind these objectives, and be able to competently articulate these reasons with *strong, clear, power words.*

Let's say you leave Ms. B a voicemail. Don't be surprised if she doesn't call back right away, because managers simply can't get to every call. But you've established yourself as an effective speaker who can get to the point, so you'll most likely be remembered next week when you follow up with another call. (In this case, persistence pays.) In any case, a concise and articulate outline will help you make a clear statement that will help you ask for exactly what you need.

Know this information at all times. Make copies of this outline format and carry it with you if necessary. Whether you need to confront a friend, make a pitch to an employer, or ask for a promotion, learning to formulate your thoughts in a pattern will make you a better communicator.

## PRODUCTIVE CHIT-CHAT

You may find yourself in a work-related social situation and feel confused about how to behave. Perhaps the prospective employer wants to meet you over coffee, or once you snag the job you're asked to attend a reception. There are certain individuals who are petrified of meeting new people and others who can maneuver around any casual conversation. If you're in the first category and find mingling intimidating, here are a few tips to help you manage when you need to.

First, before you arrive at your event destination, consider the group you'll be with for the next several hours. Naturally, you'll talk about different topics depending on the crowd you meet. Are they the newsy, read-a-lot types? You'll want to be sure to check the morning headlines to beef up your bank of current event issues to kick around. You surely wouldn't want to be the only one who is unaware of a major event that just happened yesterday.

There are certain issues most people can identify with that fall in the safe small-talk zone. When striking up a conversation with someone you're meeting for the first time, stay away from anything antagonistic, argumentative, or controversial. (It's best to take the "no politics or religion" stance.) Stick to broad topics like cultural events or local news. If you're in a group setting, ask how the guests met the host and how long they've known each other. This opens the door for more information you can build on as you continue your dialogue: "You met in graduate school? What was your major?" This approach is nothing more than the old find a crack and dig principle.

Asking open-ended questions is key. If you ask a yes-or-no question, you might simply get a yes or a no answer and have to fumble for another inquiry. Carrying the conversation can be tortuous when the one you're conversing with is not talkative. But if you're adept at asking the right kinds of question, you can get even the most timid individual to take your bait and engage.

People can feel intimidated communicating with a superior, yet even the most high-powered executive likes to talk about her kids at a social get-together. Asking her what her children are up to during the vacation season will break the ice as she personably answers your question. Other icebreakers include reports about recent or upcoming trips, a new restaurant discovery, or an informal review of a book recently read or a film just seen. You can either pose a question to your new acquaintance or simply declare how you've just seen a thought-provoking movie, which will prime the pump for more interaction.

Other openers include:

- Questions about where the other guest grew up and which school he or she attended.
- What kind of plans he or she has for the summer.
- What type of sports he or she enjoys.
- Is summer a busy season at work or does he or she find the tone to be more laid back?

No matter how relaxed the function is or how comfortable you perceive the relationship to be, there are still off-limit questions. Never ask delicate questions or bring up issues in violation of someone's privacy. For instance, obviously stay away from asking about his divorce or property settlement. Remember, there are always taboo topics when meeting new people or speaking with individuals with whom you do not share a personal relationship, and its best to consider how the other person is going to feel about your questions before you ask.

Other openers you want to avoid:

- How much do you make?
- Is your jewelry real?
- What's your political affiliation?
- What did you pay for your house?
- What's your sexual orientation?
- Real or implants?

If you find yourself the subject of one of these inappropriate inquiries, deflect it by stating, "I make more than you think but less than what I'm worth," and change the subject by asking a question of the other person. Keep in mind that some people are just socially inept, and although you may take offense to certain

## cheat sheet

Do use power and action verbs.

Do be comfortable speaking with a live person rather than only corresponding via e-mail.

Do project a can-do attitude.

Do ask for what you want; don't ramble.

Do make small talk about broad topics such as cultural events—not controversial topics.

questions, they probably weren't intended to cause you any grief.

One important thing to consider as you mingle with less familiar people: most people want to feel worthy of others' time and interest. When you make small talk, being respectful and making eye contact is an important part of any conversation. There's nothing worse than speaking with someone who is checking out the next person with whom they want to chat or looking around to see who may be more interesting. Don't be one of those people! When you ask questions with sincerity, you indicate that you're actually paying attention.

Small talk doesn't need to be a big problem. You'll find the more you mingle the easier it will be. Casual chatter doesn't just happen; it's created. ■

## CHAPTER 10

# Unspoken Signs

## KEEP BODY LANGUAGE IN CHECK

"Eye rolling
is one of the
nonverbal
signs that
is pretty
much always
aggressive. Do
you disagree?"

STEVE
WATTS

Actions speak louder than words. Even though you may know your job and are comfortable with your verbal communication, if your body language doesn't support all of this, it will be detrimental to your career. Why? Because most people believe nonverbal communication conveys most of the information in an actual message.

For example, many of us tilt our heads while we listen to someone speak; we think it indicates we're engaged in the conversation. But the tilting may actually imply you're in agreement, even if you're not. Research also shows that silence indicates either a need for approval, a fear of loss of approval, or a fear of disapproval. When you remain silent, you appear to be passive or lacking the knowledge to intellectually contribute to a discussion.

So whether it's at work or when you talk to peers, friends, or anyone else—you need to convey (and often reinforce) your messages with your nonverbal language. This includes pauses, inflections, eye contact, what you do with your hands, posture, when you choose to speak, facial expressions . . . the list goes on. This chapter will help you realize what you need to be aware of when communicating with your interviewer.

## EYE SEE YOU

Eye contact is a sure sign of confidence, as well as respect, honesty, and genuineness. When you speak with someone, do you look her in the eye? Do you have the confidence to do so? If this is a problem area for you, make a conscious effort to practice little by little.

It is hard to talk to someone who doesn't look you in the eye. You become more preoccupied with why he isn't making eye contact than with what he's saying. Why won't he look me in the eye? Is he lying? Is he insecure? Do I have food in my teeth? Eye contact regulates the flow of communication and creates a connection between those in conversation. It conveys interest, concern, warmth, and credibility. It exudes confidence. Make a point of practicing eye contact at all costs—even if it means going outside of your comfort zone. Remember, just as with everything else in life, the more you do it, the more confident you will become. And being confident will make eye contact easier—you don't have anything to hide, and you can face anyone and anything head on.

## POSTURE

Unfortunately, our mothers may actually have had a point when they told us, "Stand up straight!" and "Don't slouch!" Just like good eye contact and sophisticated language, good posture really says, "I'm confident."

Think about when you catch a person with horrible posture really hunched over. Don't you envision going over and pulling the person's shoulders back? (Not that you would ever do such a thing, but admit it, you know you want to!)

But seeing someone hunched over really does make most of us stand up taller. And standing up taller instantly brings out confidence. (Try it right now—lift your head, put your shoulders back, arch your lower back, and stand up straight. Feel the difference?) The body should be long and straight.

Now examine your posture in this position. Does it look stiff or relaxed? Do you look tense (as though you're trying too hard to hold the position) or do you look natural? Practice good posture so you appear comfortable . . . it really does make a difference!

Also, it's better for your posture (and you) to breathe from the diaphragm. To breathe properly, the stomach should move out and back, rather than the shoulders moving up and down. Air moves better through the lungs when breathing through the diaphragm.

**ADVICE FROM THE CORNER OFFICE**
Susan Sellani-Hosage, a senior manager in human resources, gives this tip: "When interviewing, a candidate's body language says almost as much as his words. Someone slouching in the chair telling you how energetic and ambitious he is doesn't create quite the same impression as the individual who is sitting at the edge of his seat leaning forward with anticipation about the opportunity."

## SILENCE SPEAKS

When you are silent or disengaged during a work meeting or interview, or even a social conversation, you may be perceived as disinterested or lacking the knowledge to intellectually contribute to the discussion. Your silence can and will limit the respect others will have for you—and it limits the wonderful contributions you could add to the project at hand! Remaining silent can also be perceived as just plain old-fashioned rude. People want to engage in conversation, and if you aren't a participant, they could ascertain you just don't want to talk to them. This silence can be detrimental in making a good first impression.

You also don't want to be a chatterbox, but make sure that your voice is heard when it counts: during an interview, in the boardroom, or whenever you have knowledge that will positively contribute to the conversation. This will showcase your knowledge and confidence and will force your interviewer to view you as someone who could be an important team member. You want to talk to the person and tell him or her all your great accomplishments concisely but thoroughly.

## DON'T JUST NOD

There are also nonverbal messages you can send without meaning to communicate what is interpreted. For example, when you nod your head, you may assume that you're letting the other person know you're listening, but most people take nodding to mean that you're agreeing with them. Also, as already noted, if you tilt your head thinking you are conveying curiosity, it can convey confusion and make you seem unintelligent. A good way to remember this is to think of the saying "Someone who keeps his head up straight looks like he has his head on straight." However, if you do agree, by all means nod away!

## OTHER NOTABLE GESTURES

To emphasize the importance of gestures, here are a few more nonverbal messages to examine in your communication. Incidentally, these actions aren't always taken this way, but it is worth noting these are common interpretations that can be harmful to the impression you're putting out to your interviewer.

*Folding arms:* Gives off a perception of being defensive, closed off, or bored.

*Pointing:* This can be negative because it appears to be authoritative or bossy (especially in a situation where you want to appear approachable).

*Smiles:* A fake smile implies insincerity. A sincere smile is one of those things you just know when you see, and it is contagious and very, very genuine.

*Also*—you definitely don't want to play with your hair, tug at your clothes, or pick at your nails.

These nonverbal messages don't communicate professionalism! This is the last message you want to send to a potential employer. Nonverbal communication not only brings credibility to spoken words, it reflects a proper state of mind. Do you talk with your hands? Sometimes it is necessary to emphasize the point, but it can look like you're karate-chopping your way into the conversation. Do you play with your hair? This is always a "no"; it indicates insecurity and immaturity.

These are all pieces of communication that you need to analyze to discover what messages you are sending (or not sending) to your peers and supervisors. If you do any of these or myriad other gestures when answering a question asked by the interviewer, it can also indicate that you are not telling the truth. So, as silly as it sounds, practice your verbal—and *nonverbal*—answers to interview questions in front of a mirror so you can see exactly what messages you are sending.

## WHAT ALL OF THIS MEANS IN AN INTERVIEW

All of this information is important to you because hiring managers will be evaluating your nonverbal communication during the interview process. From the time you enter the lobby (do you sit quietly, are you chewing your nails, looking annoyed because they are running late?) to the time you shake hands and leave the interview, your nonverbal cues are all taken into consideration and give your interviewer clues as to the type of person you are and whether your actions reinforce your words.

**ADVICE FROM THE CORNER OFFICE**
Joanne Coghill, assistant vice president human resources for a large mortgage bank, says, "Perception is significant. Be professional and focused. Turn off your computer/phone device. Fidgeting or being engaged with your phone, iPod, etc., is distracting and rude while interviewing and/or talking with execs."

Nonverbal communication is crucial because not only does it bring credibility to spoken words, it reflects a person's state of mind. You can analyze your interviewer's nonverbal communication as well to let you know how your meeting went and if you need to give more information while you're there. For example, when an interviewer asks you a question, her nonverbal cues will tell you if you're answering what she asked. Watch your interviewer's face for clues to see if you are giving the answer she is looking for.

If she looks confused or puzzled, stop what you are saying and ask her to clarify the question. This way you can transition your current answer to the answer she is searching for. If she starts to look away while you are talking, decide if your answer is too long or if you are rambling. If so, wrap it up! ∎

## cheat sheet

Don't be quiet.

Do make eye contact throughout any conversation.

Do sit up straight; you don't want to slump in your chair.

Don't miss clues from others about whether they understand what you're saying.

Do make sure your nonverbal and verbal communications convey the same message.

Don't neglect analyzing what message your nonverbals are sending.

## CHAPTER 11

# Adjust Your Jargon

## ADDRESSING DIFFERENT PERSONALITY TYPES

> "The words you choose to say something are just as important as the decision to speak."
>
> AUTHOR UNKNOWN

By now you know to use proper grammar and act professionally when talking with an interviewer. In this chapter you'll find a few tricks to help you read your interviewer.

Different people have different personalities—seems obvious, right? But if you can learn to assess people's personalities when they seek information, it will lead to communication success.

In simple terms, to get what you want, adapt your voice and tone of speech to suit the person from whom you need something. You would speak differently to a small child, to a boyfriend or girlfriend, and to a supervisor. You would not use the same tone of voice, a similar vocabulary, or an equal approach with all of them. The same goes for individuals who interview you. While there should be a level of professionalism while speaking to anyone who is a potential supervisor, each interviewer still has his or her own personality. If you can determine what type of personality your interviewer has, your communication will be even more successful!

## THE ASSESSMENT

There are many different assessments to determine personalities. We like (and have found great personal success) with the DiSC personality system (*www.discprofile.com*). With this method, personalities are explained and tips given for successful communication.

With DiSC, there are four personality types. Once you understand these types, you can use this knowledge to profile people in any situation and can set yourself up for successful communication after conversing with someone for just a few minutes. For example, when talking to a recruiter who explains things with great attention to detail, you can ascertain that this person is most likely looking for detailed answers in return. But when talking to someone who is more of a "bottom-line only" person, then you should keep answers to bare details.

Understanding and tailoring your conversations makes you appear knowledgeable and articulate because you are adapting—not compromising—communication to specific situations. Here is a basic overview; you'll find more detailed information at their website.

The way the DiSC personality model and the four basic personality traits were explained to us was with a mountain scenario. Say there's a mountain, and the team, the group, the family, or whoever, has to get over the mountain. This is the mission. Each personality type has its own method to get the group over the mountain.

## THE TYPES

According to the DiSC profile, the four basic traits look something like this:

- The D personalities (dominance) are the ones who get everyone over the mountain no matter the obstacles in the way. D people are dependable; they are leaders. If a D person has been given a task, then a task he or she shall do. Not always, but sometimes there can be little regard for feelings, and there's no time for niceties. These are bottom-line people. With a D at the helm, everyone, without a doubt, will get over the mountain. Ds are determined and aggressive, but they can also be innovative and creative; they are leaders, and they get the job done.
- The I personalities (influencers) get everyone over the mountain, but I people take the "yay team" approach. They are great motivators, appreciate everyone's hard work, and want everyone to have fun and feel good going over the mountain. They are persuasive and optimistic. In addition, they like to be told what a great job they're doing in leading everyone; they love to be recognized, rewarded, and praised. Reward systems work wonders for I people. It's just the wiring of their personality.
- The S personalities (steadiness) question the whole mountain scenario: Why the heck do I have to go over this mountain when I'm perfectly happy right here?! S personalities don't like change. It isn't that they won't "do" change, they will. They just like the existing harmony, and favor the steadiness of things, and change disrupts the steadiness.

- The C personalities (conscientiousness or compliance) will get you over the mountain, but it will be via intricate steps. At approximately 1:34 P.M., they will be at quadrant F of the graphed chart. From that quadrant, they will move four steps to the left, which will put them closer to quadrant B on the highly detailed map. Every single, solitary step will be thorough, well thought out, and completely detailed. There isn't room for error; it's all too meticulous. They get everyone over the mountain because of precise planning, rules, and regulations.

The DiSC system is easy because it helps put conversation styles into four distinct compartments, but there can also be many different combinations with the DiSC system. You may have a dominant D personality with a bit of I thrown in, so you still are able to "yay team" them while concisely giving the bottom-line numbers. You may be dominant in one and have just a touch of another section, or it may be a 50/50 split—each personality is unique. Just by recognizing that there are different personalities that need to be adapted to, the communication awareness process opens up tremendously.

Think about this, too. Do you have a friend, boss, or professor whom you know to only ask a question to when you have enough time to hear the answer? This person *has* to give you a detailed answer, even if it is a yes or no question! To this person, though, there are no such things as yes or no questions. He's a C. He wants to give you the details behind the answer. And it's okay; it is just the way he's wired.

You usually can tell if someone is a C after simply asking one or two questions. Have you ever been at a restaurant where you asked the waiter a question and he gave you a long-drawn-out answer? So you know at the beginning of dinner not to ask any more conversational questions for the rest of the meal.

Maybe you have a friend, teacher, or parent to whom you want to tell a story, but she *only* wants the pertinent info? She's a D. She may interrupt you mid-story and ask for your point or try to rush you. If she is the one who asked you for information, she may either ask another question or just bluntly ask again for *only* the info she needs.

If you work with someone or have a friend who is always the one you or others go to when a word of encouragement is needed, you know an I. She's the person who is always there to cheer you on, and let you know what a great job you're doing. I people love giving out praise, but also like to receive it. So, if you work with an I, it's best to praise or recognize her, too. For example, before asking for something, be sure to say thanks for a moment of training she gave to you off to the side, or tell her how great her presentation was in the meeting the other day.

And if you have a friend who is the last on the block to get the new iPod (financial reasons not withstanding), doesn't switch out of his routine, or doesn't like to "rock the boat," you're conversing with an S. He likes the steadiness of his life. He doesn't need to change, because everything works–and he knows *how* it works—"just fine."

### In the Interview

Use this knowledge to help you read your interviewer and land a job, too! Pay attention from the very beginning to how he speaks. Is he curt and abrupt but still professional? Is he detailed? Maybe he makes mention of a new change in the company "that takes some getting use to." Pay attention to these cues and you'll know how to tailor your talk!

If you end up with a C-personality interviewer, you can't avoid asking questions for fear of long-drawn-out answers! But you can determine which questions are the most relevant since each question may get an extremely long answer and you only have a certain amount of time allotted for your interview. Ask your most relevant questions or the ones you *really* want the answers to during this particular interview.

Also, realize that you also now know your interviewer is looking for details from you when you answer his questions. He likes details, so be specific!

If you get an interviewer who is a D-personality type, you know to answer with only short, professional answers. You should still sell your job skills, but answer *concisely*! She wants only bottom-line info.

Should your interviewer be an I, you'll know because you'll almost be able to feel him wanting you to do well. (No, he won't "help" you, but he is more optimistic and expressive in demeanor.) Therefore, he is especially, more so than other interviewers, looking for optimism, enthusiasm, and someone who is outgoing during the interview process.

The S interviewer will have a cooperative, stable demeanor. She'll be diplomatic and consistent. You may be able to pick this up in the way she describes the culture of the company; does she make a point of mentioning the changes and, perhaps, "the adjustments needed to make the change happen?" You may also be able to determine an S by the power of elimination. The other three are so distinctive and, if you don't feel the person is dominant in one of them, opt for S.

Remember, once you get the job, you'll want to continue to understand what coworkers, managers, and clients want in terms of communication. You need to adapt to and assess these different personalities. Again, these are basic guidelines, but they will help.

For example, when walking into your detail-oriented manager's office, be prepared with each step and intricate detail for whatever project, plan, or proposal that is being addressed. You know he wants specific, detailed information. These personality types like step-by-step instructions; they enjoy doing intricate tasks.

If you are walking into the office of a "bottom-line only" (D) person, then bring only the barest of details and the most accurate bottom-line number available. Be firm and direct. If you know something won't work, politely offer another solution in its place. Focus on goals, objectives, and results, and be brief and to the point. Have the answers (or know where to find them) when confronting this person about any projects.

And if someone on your team doesn't like change (S type), make sure she is understood, both by you and by other team members. Some people really don't want to go over the mountain. They *will* go over; they just don't like it (because they like the steadiness of the current situation). These people need time to process information and the changes ahead of them, because what if the other side of the mountain isn't great?

When trying to relate to a person who likes to be encouraged (I type), be sure to give recognition and encouragement. Use a congenial voice tone to confirm a positive working relationship. Allow this person to praise you back and express himself verbally.

The DiSC method isn't foolproof. There have been times where, no matter how well versed we are—and we have given countless assessments to managers and employees within various companies—that we just couldn't determine someone's personality profile. But overall, it really does help to determine the appropriate way to enter into a conversation.

### Know Yourself

Adapting to someone else (the employer) may be much easier to understand if you know who you are. You can even take your own online quiz *(www.discprofile.com)* to determine your personality type for sure. (The website offers several variations: for work, for teens, for leaders.) Although, chances are, you probably know if you are someone who needs praise (I), a detailed chart (C), want to keep things steady (S), or isn't worried about making friends as long as the job gets done (D).

For example, if you are a "bottom-line only" person, you have a tendency to be curt and abrupt and get the job done no matter what, even if you lose friends along the way. Acknowledge this and understand that not everyone will relate. You will work with I people; your boss may even have that personality type. They want encouragement and enthusiasm.

And if you're an S type, recognize it, too. Be self-aware because if change is upon you, and you're aware of how you deal with it, then you can also be careful with the change and understand it so it isn't a scary piece of life.

Acknowledge who you are, do not change who you are, and understand that successful people are those who can relate to all types. If you understand yourself and that other types exist, then this recognition will improve communication. This is especially true when trying to land a job!

It's important to realize that none of these personalities are bad or have to be changed. Ideally, everyone should probably strive to be a little of everything for a well-rounded personality. But recognizing the traits as they are now in people makes communication so much easier because you can adapt your communication style and tailor interactions for both professional and personal success. Adaptation is key. You are your own generation, and many employers are beginning to understand this. But you will have to overcome generational differences to land a job, and understanding the different ways to interact and communicate will give you a significant advantage over your competition. ■

## cheat sheet

Do know that there are different personalities with different communication styles.

Don't assume everyone likes every piece of detail you want to share.

Don't neglect to determine your own personality type so you can adapt your own speaking.

## CHAPTER 12

# Ask Away

## INTERVIEW Q&A MADE EASY

> "The main thing to do is relax and let your talent do the work."
>
> **CHARLES BARKLEY**

Answering your interviewer's questions intelligently is crucial to selling the recruiter on your skills and ability to do the job with ease. Preparing your answers to common interview questions ahead of time is a great way to make sure you're giving the best answers possible. It is equally important to have information already prepared when you are asked, "Do you have any questions?"

Why? Because in addition to portraying yourself as the best candidate for the job, you want to use the interview to determine if the company is going to be a good fit for you. You should completely understand what a particular position offers because then you'll be less likely to ignore the realities of the job or company and not find yourself in a place you dislike.

## YOU'LL PROBABLY BE ASKED . . .

### Who Are You?

Many interviewers open by asking, "Tell me about yourself." This has potential for either disaster or a job-landing answer summarizing who you are and why you are a good candidate for the position.

You want to give your elevator speech. It is called this because if you're riding in an elevator for thirty seconds and have to communicate all the details about something before the doors open, you need to be able to summarize your goals, plans, and ideas immediately. And you want to be prepared to answer this question immediately, too.

Have something prepared for your elevator speech that is short and concise, but be careful not to sound rehearsed. Here's an example:

> Professionally, I am extremely skilled in technology and am able to navigate troubleshooting problems with ease. I am extremely organized and possess a sense of urgency. Personally, I am an avid runner and participated in last year's city marathon.

You want to throw skills out there as well as immediately humanize yourself and toss out a memorable something about you. Chances are the marathon running (or hockey playing or your semester of studying abroad) will stand out and help to give you an identity in the interviewer's mind.

**ADVICE FROM THE CORNER OFFICE**

Keith Oreson, executive vice president of the *Fortune* 500 company Advance Auto Parts, Inc., consistently asks potential employees:

- What values have you formed as a result of your early family background? "It shows what really is at the essence of an individual and what may guide their behavior in the workplace."
- What is the best piece of constructive criticism you've received from a boss? Why did you get it and what did you do about it? "This gives insight into potential developmental areas and whether the person is open to feedback and improving themselves."

## Scenario Questions

Many interviewers use a technique called behavioral interviewing. This entails asking questions in search of a specific response. For example, "Tell me a time you went above and beyond for a project." The person is asking for a particular time, so be sure to provide one!

*Bad answer:* Oh, I do it all the time. Every time I'm on a project I always do more than my share.

*Good answer:* Senior year we did a group project about marketing a new product, and even though we were on track and had prepared the necessary information, someone recommended a seminar that might help us, so I contacted the facilitator and interviewed her as part of the project for additional credibility and information.

If an interviewer asks any question seeking out an example of particular time, scenario, or example, be sure to give it. Even if you have to stop and take a moment to think about it, do so in order to come up with a specific example. Those who give the generic, blanketed "every time" answer usually don't make it past the first interviewer. Why? Because if you really did these things, you would *definitely* have a specific answer.

**ADVICE FROM THE CORNER OFFICE**
**Julie Grass, HR professional and founder of The Momentum Group, recommends, when answering interview questions:**

- **Avoid criticizing your prior bosses and colleagues.**
- **When you focus on the negative, interviewers may think you are someone who finds fault in and blames others.**
- **And if you bash previous employers, why wouldn't you bash them?**

### The Good and the Bad

Everybody knows to be prepared to answer, "What are your strengths?" and "What are your weakness/areas of development?" But *how* do you answer this? Don't take these questions for granted and not prepare. Quality answers will separate you from the rest of the candidates who are answering these standards, too.

Have three answers prepared to illustrate your strengths, which can include follow-through on projects, quest for learning, prior knowledge you bring to the company, a sense of urgency on projects, communication skills, knowledge of particular skills, organization. Whatever characteristics you choose to use to describe yourself, be sure to have an example to back them up.

EXAMPLES:

- "I am extremely organized. At my internship, I created an entirely new filing system that included color-coded folders."
- "I have excellent follow-through. I received a commendation at my previous employer for consistently following through on all customer orders."

For weaknesses, which many refer to as "areas of development," again, have three prepared. The trick is to answer with a weakness that is actually a strength or an area that is easily correctable.

EXAMPLES

- "While I am familiar with Excel, I'd like to learn to be more proficient in it, and right now I'm just not extremely skilled in this application." (This is an acceptable answer *only* if the position isn't calling for someone completely proficient in Excel!)
- "I am obviously a new college grad, and therefore my lack of work experience in terms of years within the field can hold me at a disadvantage."
- "Some say I am too organized because I like to have everything in its place."
- "I have a tendency to be a perfectionist."

See how it works?

### Why You?

When an interviewer asks why a company should hire you, use this as a perfect opportunity to really sell yourself. Say what makes you special, state your experience, and, for good measure, also throw in your willingness and ability to learn quickly and how your previous experience would greatly benefit this company. You could say something like this:

> Because this position is calling for someone who is a good salesperson with the desire to move into management. Even though I only worked part time at my internship in sales while at school, I was always within the highest sales per hour category when comparing the hours worked versus how much I sold per hour. I also see myself pursuing a career in management. I held a leadership position in the Xyz organization and was successful in knowing how to motivate and inspire those around me.

**ADVICE FROM THE CORNER OFFICE**
La'Trise Smith, assistant vice president of human resources at Huntington Bank, says that her favorite question to ask an applicant is "If a coworker or manager had to describe you, what would they say?" This shows a sense of self-awareness on the part of the applicant.

### What Did You Like or Dislike?

When asked what you liked or disliked about your last job, be honest as long as you aren't badmouthing someone. (True story, in an actual interview we conducted, this girl said she wanted to leave because "My boss was a total b----" . . . uh oh!)

# CLASS NOTES

Courtney, 24

Courtney graduated from Duke University with a degree in International Studies. She hadn't completely decided what she wanted to do careerwise, but the jobs that most interested her were looking for more experience (seven to ten years) than she had just out of college. So she went into it knowing she wanted to find **a starter job** to get one year of experience to be able to later get a position she truly wanted. She submitted her resume online to many entry-level positions and was hired at a large online job placement company where she sold online advertisements to various companies.

She found it to be a very regimented, controlled environment, and after the one year she did leave. "For the next position I knew I needed to spend more time making sure it was a work environment that I wanted to be in," she says. Her managers at this first job out of college were not much older than she was and there was a fine line between friend and manager. When she applied for the next position, she went in with the goal of looking **to work for older, more experienced managers** who could teach her and help her advance in the field.

"I like to know 'why,'" she says. "I want to work with those who have the experience to tell me this." Courtney now works in sales for one of the largest transportation companies in the country.

Her advice to those looking for their first job out of college is to take the time to determine whether or not it is a working environment where you can learn, where **managers are also mentors**. And, she advises, do not ever turn down an interview. "Even if I was sure I wouldn't take the job, I always took the interview for practice . . . plus an interview can change your mind about what you think the job really is," she says. "Take advantage of all opportunities and know what you're looking for!"

Chances are, since this is your first or second job out of school, it's easy (and honest) to say you are looking for more opportunity, challenges, and greater potential to grow within a company.

### Where Are You Going?

This is the dreaded "Where do you see yourself in five years" question. Think about this . . . where *do* you see yourself? Be realistic. Although if you see yourself backpacking through the Andes, don't be too honest! You're probably not going to be a VP, but you may very well be in a middle-management position. If this is what you want, say it. If you want to work on larger, national accounts or even head them up, say this. Know what you want and have some goals prepared.

### Why Here?

Employers want to know why you want to work at their company. This is probably somewhat of a test to see what kind of research you have done about their organization. So if you go into the interview knowing their background information or potential for growth, it shows true interest to the person who is interviewing you.

EXAMPLE:

- "I want to work for this company because of the large growth potential. In the last three years the stock price has risen four points on average per year. This tells me it is a company that is thriving and is being run by successful leaders."
- "I want to work for this company because of the low turnover rate of employees. Obviously people love working here because of the corporate culture and the quality of work employees are able to contribute."

## HAVE EXAMPLE AFTER EXAMPLE READY

Be very familiar with all you have accomplished and be prepared to answer with specific examples:

- Why are you a team player? (Give an example of being on a team.)
- What motivates you? (Know yourself—if it's recognition, monetary, time off, awards, doing a good job, or promotional opportunities, be prepared with an honest answer.)
- What are challenges you have overcome? (Perhaps it is projects in school, taking on a position in the student government, sorority or fraternity or at your internship; perhaps it is something personal.)
- What is your work ethic? (Talk about staying late to finish a project with a specific deadline, or contributing above and beyond to a project.)
- How do you describe fun at the workplace? (Be careful here. You want to answer with camaraderie and a team-playing spirited answer.)
- How did you resolve a particular conflict while working on the job or on a school project?
- How would a prior boss and/or a professor describe you? (Use positive, concise adjectives with a small description of why.)
- How did you handle a stressful situation or a time when something went wrong at the last minute?

## PRACTICE MAKES PERFECT

Practice your answers over and over, but know there will be questions unique to a particular company, interviewer, or position that may throw you off. If this happens, go ahead and take a moment to collect your thoughts before answering. It's okay to take a minute to think—it shows attention and conscientiousness over details.

## ASK, ASK, ASK

When the recruiter is done asking you questions, he'll ask what you'd like to know. After you've convinced the recruiter that you're the person for the job, you need to make sure that the job fits you, too.

This is the time to jump in and interview the company. When a candidate and job connect, it needs to be with a mutual understanding that both will thrive.

### ADVICE FROM THE CORNER OFFICE

Julie Grass, HR professional and founder of the Momentum Group, says, "Interviewers can learn a lot about you based on the questions you ask. For instance, asking 'What are the biggest challenges your company is facing?' and 'What, in your opinion, makes you different from your competitors?' shows that you are interested in the big picture. Stay away from *only* asking questions like 'How soon can I expect a raise or promotion?' This suggests self-interest only."

Don't be afraid to ask questions to determine if you want the job. Hiring managers are usually impressed when you take advantage of the time to ask about the company; it shows interest! But questions should be well thought out, specific, and designed to provide an accurate picture of what life on the job really will be. Here is a sample of possible questions to ask, but remember, these questions are guidelines; some may or may not be appropriate for your particular position.

- How would you describe the company culture?
- What is the vision of the department over the course of the next year? The next three?
- What is the organizational structure within the company?
- What is your style of management?
- How are new company initiatives/programs/policies communicated?
- Why is this position open? Is there any opportunity for advancement?
- How am I evaluated in this position? Is there a reward system used?
- What do you enjoy about working here? How did your employment experience bring you to this company?
- What is a typical working day? Week?
- What qualities do you think a person needs to be successful in this job? Company?
- What is the employee turnover rate?
- Does the company believe in work/life balance?
- What is the branding strategy of the company?
- Is it possible to talk with other supervisors or subordinates within the department? (If you're not already set up to interview with others.)

- What is the training program for the position?
- Is there diversity within the company?
- What type of decisions will I be responsible for in this position?
- Is the workplace a fun, motivating atmosphere?
- Is there anything else that I should tell you about my qualifications, in terms of requirements of the position not already discussed?

In addition to this, ask your interviewer about her career history or her experience with the company. People love to talk about themselves, and the fact that you seem interested will demonstrate your interest in her as a person.

**ADVICE FROM THE CORNER OFFICE**
Susan Sellani-Hosage, a senior manager in human resources, reminds: Never ask what the job pays. It doesn't matter if the salary is a million dollars if you don't get it. There will be a more appropriate time to discuss the compensation, and your bargaining position will be greatly improved once you know you're the top candidate.

Asking questions is important, and the above questions give you a great place to start. However, the most important question you can ask is, "What qualities does the person you hire need to be successful in this job? Who are you looking to hire for this position?"

This question is especially important because you want to listen intently to learn who and what qualities they want for this position. Soak it in. Then, at the end of the interview, when the interviewer asks, "Is there anything you'd like to add?," you'll have the PERFECT opportunity to recite back everything they just said about who and what they want.

Example: The interviewer says, "This person must know how to manage time, be creative, and work independently to meet deadlines. We're looking for someone who really understands the concepts of 'XYZ.'"

Now, hold on to this information and when asked, "Is there anything you'd like to add?" you'll say:

> "I just want you to know that I'm very interested in this position and am completely confident in my ability to contribute. With all the activities I participated in during college, time management skills are something I have mastered. I always meet deadlines and am very interested in working on projects such as XYZ, because I understand them so well."

See? This plays back into what the interviewer specifically said he or she wants in the ideal candidate. ■

## cheat sheet

Do go to an interview prepared to answer questions.

Don't give generalized answers to questions asking for a specific example.

Don't blurt out the answer without taking a minute to collect your thoughts.

Do prepare a list of questions to ask the interviewer.

Do research the company prior to your interview.

Don't answer questions with long-winded sentences.

## CHAPTER 13

# Make Your Mark

## LEAVE A LASTING IMPRESSION

"All that matters is the ending, it's the most important part of the story, and this one is very good. This one is perfect."

JOHNNY DEPP

As "Mort Rainey" in *Secret Window*

Know that an interview is over when it's over! Be aware of the "we're done now" cues, lest you overstay your welcome. This is often where applicants sabotage themselves because, until this point, your questions and answers have been well prepared, your goals are firmly expressed, and you have likely been engaged in a great conversation. So exit with grace.

**WHAT TO ASK BEFORE YOU LEAVE**

Before your goodbye handshake, you want to be sure you have acquired the pertinent information you'll need down the road. Because, armed with appropriate knowledge, you can conduct a thorough and impressive follow-up once your interview is complete.

1. Be sure you have obtained the correct names and job titles of all the people who interviewed you. This is easy to do if you remember to ask each

person who played a significant role in your interview for a business card. If you fail to do this, you'll have to call the receptionist as soon as you get home and ask for the correct spelling of everyone's name and title, which could be nothing short of a headache.

2. Ask the employer when he or she expects to make the hiring decision. Whether it's three days or three weeks, you'll be forewarned so you can keep in contact within this timeline.

## TAKE A HINT

Here are some clues to watch and listen for to alert you to the fact you've come to the finish line:

- When your interviewer has stood up, stand up with her and get ready to extend a handshake.
- When your interviewer says something like, "I appreciate your interest, we'll look over your file and get back to you."
- When you hear, "Okay, thank you for coming, we'll be in touch."

At this point, stand up and give the impression that you understand your time is up. This is not the time to think, "but I'm still not finished telling you about myself" or "I forgot to mention a few other things you should know about me." From this moment forward, unless you're answering more questions as you walk out, any other embellishments may count against you. Whatever you feel you may have neglected to mention can be jotted in the note you will be sending within the next few hours.

As you walk out, engage in small talk, but use it to your advantage. If you know that your prospective boss is a sports fan, chat about a game you plan to attend. You want your interviewer to know that you have social skills and the ability to carry on a conversation. Be sure to prepare for your grand finale, so you can conclude your interview with poise and self-assurance.

**ADVICE FROM THE CORNER OFFICE**
Deb Kintigh, corporate director of human resources at Driftwood Hospitality Management LLC, says, "The end of the interview should not come as a surprise if you're listening closely. You will most likely be asked what questions you have and the interviewer may tell you what the next steps are in the selection process. If not, don't be afraid to ask."

## SEND A NOTE

The interview is over, what a relief! Not so fast. Just because you showed up for your appointment, endured the challenging questions, and made it safely back home does not mean you can sit back and wait for a job offer. Your work is not finished just because you've completed the interview.

Remember, there are probably numerous applicants vying for the same position, so you want to make sure you rise above the rest. Before you do anything else, once you get home, sit down and write a thank-you note to each person with whom you interviewed. Ideally, everyone who interviewed you should receive a note within two days of your meeting. Like every other stage in this job hunt, this is an important step to grab the position you want!

Even with something as simple as a thank-you note, you should take the time to write it well and make sure names are spelled correctly. Sending a note with misspelled names and bad grammar will certainly reduce your standing as a qualified candidate. There are three types of thank-you notes from which to choose: a formal letter on the same stationery as your resume, an informal note card, or an e-mail thanks.

The handwritten note card is often considered the most personable and is appropriate if you feel you hit it off with an interviewer. If handwritten, your note should be legible, but a typed letter with a handwritten signature is fine if your penmanship is horrendous. Some people suggest soliciting the help of a friend with good handwriting skills, but we don't advise this. Once you get hired, your new boss will soon realize that you have lousy penmanship, and the fact you've had someone else cover for you is less than honest.

Obviously, a formal letter is the most conservative, so go this route if you're applying at a traditional organization such as a law firm or a bank. The e-mail thank-you note is the most informal, and if pressed for time (if your interviewer told you the hiring decision will be made within two days), you'll want to choose this format.

The note should reiterate your interest in the job and reaffirm some of your strong points. Perhaps you can mention how, now that you've seen the office environment first hand, you are more confident your skills can be valuable to the company. You want your interviewer to view this connective expression as another one of your assets of being responsible, courteous, and thoughtful.

The note should be casual but direct. Definitely use the recipient's full name, and make the effort to send a different note to everyone. The notes can be similar, but make deliberate distinctions so it doesn't look like you mindlessly issued the same form letter if the recipients happen to compare notes about you after they receive your note.

As salutations go, if your interviewer introduced herself to you as Ms. Hughes, then you should address the note this way. If she said "please call me Carol," feel free to write, "Dear Carol." Once you've actually made a personal association, you will probably want to use a less formal tone. The casual note should look something like this:

July 1, 2009

Dear Carol,

It was great to meet you and interview for the sales rep position today. You gave me great information about your company and I enjoyed meeting some of the members of the sales team.

What you shared with me about your company has made me even more passionate about wanting to work with you. I am certain my strong technology skills can help the department achieve its sales goals.

I will contact you next week to see if you've made a decision.

Thank you for taking the time to meet with me and consider me for this job.

Sincerely,

Jody Jobless

The more formal note should look like this:

July 1, 2009

Dear Ms. Hughes,

Thank you for giving me the opportunity to interview for the sales rep position today. I appreciate the information you shared with me and was impressed with the others on the sales team who I had a chance to meet.

Walking through the premises and learning about your company has made me even more eager about the possibility of working with you. I am certain my strong technology skills can help the department achieve its sales goals.

I will contact you next week to see if you've made a decision.

I appreciate your time and consideration.

Sincerely,

Jody Jobless

From then on, keep in touch but don't be a pest. If you make yourself a nuisance, the hiring manager may feel that you'd be annoying to work with and pass over you. A very brief call or e-mail to touch base about every week or two is plenty if you still haven't heard back.

And as an added bonus, if you really want to impress a potential employer, ask someone on your personal or professional reference list to call or write to the person who interviewed you to reinforce his or her recommendation.

## THE FOLLOW-UP PHONE CALL

You've sent the thank-you note several days ago and the phone is still not ringing. Unless your interviewer specified a decision would be made by the fifteenth of the month and it's now the seventeenth and you haven't heard, give people a week after you mailed your letter to contact you before you follow your note with a call. Follow up with the primary interviewer as a way to show your enthusiasm for the position.

"Hi Ms. Smith, this is Jody Jobless. I interviewed with you last week and because I'm so interested in this opportunity, I thought I should follow up with you to see if you've made a hiring decision yet."

You'll likely get one of the following responses:

- You got the job.
- You did not get the job.
- The decision has not been finalized yet.

If you didn't get the job, don't let it discourage you from pressing forward and moving on to the next opportunity. It's disappointing, but you'll find another opportunity just as promising so don't lose hope. Accept the answer with grace and professionalism; you never know if you'll be interviewing for another position at this company (or with this person) at a later date.

And don't not call, presuming the interviewer must be busy and you'd be bugging her by calling. The close is always in the follow-up. Your prospective boss may be contemplating between you and someone else, unable to make a decision. Your persistence and commitment to the position will make you look like the better candidate. Interviewers really do observe who will actually follow up and the process they use to do it.

## ADVICE FROM THE CORNER OFFICE

Deb Kintigh, corporate director of human resources at Driftwood Hospitality Management LLC, recommends these steps after an interview:

### THANK-YOU NOTES:

- If the interviewer does not offer you his or her business card, ask for one. If a card is not available, write down the person's name (check for correct spelling), title, and phone number.
- Be sure you have this information for everyone you'd like to thank.
- In the age of the Internet, immediate thank-you notes are welcome and show a genuine sign of interest.
- The note should be concise, thoughtful, and sincere when thanking the interviewer for his or her time and the opportunity to learn more about the company and the position. Take a few sentences to restate your interest in the position and briefly recap your most relevant and impressive skills. When closing the letter, "Sincerely" is appropriate.
- Proofread your letter to ensure there are no mistakes or typos.

### FOLLOW-UP PHONE CALL:

- When discussing the next steps with the interviewer, it is advisable to ascertain when the company anticipates making a hiring decision. Based upon this information, you can time your follow-up phone call to again thank the interviewer for his or her time and reiterate your interest in the position.
- A word of caution: plan in advance what you want to say and keep it brief.

## PRESSED FOR TIME

Congratulations! You may have received another offer from a different company and now need get back to them about whether or not you want to take the position. If the job you're waiting to hear about is your first choice, find out if you're getting the job prior to responding to the proposal you've just received. In such a case, be frank with the hiring professionals you're waiting on, informing them of the job offer you've just received.

Here again you can make a plug for yourself by stating your first choice is to work with them, but you would appreciate an answer so you don't miss this new opportunity if they opt not to hire you. Sometimes informing a prospective employer another potential employer is pursuing you can help speed a stalling decision. If you are a worthy candidate, they may quickly choose to hire you so you don't go with another company.

But don't use this as a ploy to get a quick answer. Don't say you've been offered another position if you haven't. It just might backfire if the hiring manager of the position you really want says, "Well, we're not ready to make a choice just yet, so if you feel you need to take advantage of the offer, do so and we'll take you out of the running for our company."

## A GRACIOUS REJECTION

Even if you were turned down for the position you applied for, it is a nice touch to send another thank-you letter to express your gratitude for being considered, as well as to express your interest in future opportunities. The job may be offered to someone else who passes it up for a better offer, or the company may hire someone else who doesn't work out. It's important not to burn

## cheat sheet

Don't overstay your welcome at an interview.

Don't harass your interviewer with incessant phone calls.

Don't be rude or offensive, demanding a quick decision.

Don't stop job hunting.

Don't lie about having multiple job offers.

Do be patient; a hiring decision takes time.

Do follow up with a thank-you note to every person you met.

Do stay in touch by phone.

Do reaffirm your strengths in your thank-you note.

Don't feel hopeless if you don't get the job.

bridges because you may be offered the job after all—or recommended for a different position in later months.

It's easy to feel rejected if you were passed over, but many times another applicant had one small feature that the new employer was interested in. A refusal does not mean your talents and skills are not worthy of another good job!

If you have the emotional fortitude, you may consider placing a call to your interviewer to ask why you were declined. You can tell her you're hoping to refine your skills for the next interview opportunity and ask for advice on how you can improve your chances. This is difficult for a lot of people, because you will likely hear some offending criticisms. But think how much help this can be to you for future interviews!

Be forewarned: resist the temptation to defend yourself. Even if you don't agree with the interviewer's assessment, be courteous and thank her for sharing her observation with you. Be brave and consider the exchange to be a part of your education in your quest for the ideal job. You may be surprised at how much you learn about yourself. And you definitely don't need to do this after every interview, or with every interviewer, but if you feel that a person can share some insight, be confident enough to seek out the feedback. ∎

## CHAPTER 14

# Guts and Gratification

## NEGOTIATE YOUR WAY

> "A lot of people are afraid to say what they want. That's why they don't get what they want."
>
> MADONNA

Congratulations! You've made it through the interview process and found a company that wants you as much as you want them. The next part of the hiring process is sealing the deal: confirmation of the salary and benefits.

Knowing what you want is one thing, but getting it is another. Sometimes it's a game; sometimes it's a give and take. Either way, with the right tools, frame of mind, and confidence, you can negotiate salaries, positions, ideas you believe in, or a coveted spot on a team project.

You just need to have a strategy and know what you can offer to whomever it is you're negotiating. The idea of the whole process is to get what you want from the one who has the power to give it to you, and knowing what to say and how to say it will help you reach your goals!

## WAIT FOR THE OFFER

When negotiating salary, you really don't have too much leverage until a position has officially been offered. If you start to play hardball with salary during the second or third interview, you just may negotiate yourself out of any kind of deal—even if you are a top candidate!

Once a position is offered, however, you're free to go for it, but don't start negotiating as soon as it is offered. Listen to the offer and the compensation package and let the company know you'll get back to them after you think about it. This lets them know you're seriously considering it, that you may have other offers (they don't want to lose you so it may get them to think, too), and it serves as a prewarning that you will submit a counteroffer.

**ADVICE FROM THE CORNER OFFICE**
**Joanne Coghill, assistant vice president human resources for a large mortgage bank, offers these tips:**

- **Have your facts in line when negotiating.**
- **Ask for what is fair and be willing to compromise.**
- **Do not demand.**
- **Have a backup plan.**
- **Speak clearly.**

**THE FINE LINE**

Negotiation is expected, but you must not act entitled. This process must be fair to you and fair for the company, but don't think you don't deserve it either. This is a fine line, so walk it well.

You totally deserve every penny you are eligible to make, but you need to make sure, without doubt or hesitation, that you truly are entitled to the money. If the job description states duties worthy of $30k, don't expect to make $50k (or even $40k for that matter). It's all relative.

You can negotiate to get your fair due. If your demeanor is right, and you come across as sincere and confident, you may get what you want. You need to communicate confidence, without overstepping into conceit. And remember, it is a different generation you are negotiating with, too. They want hard work first, money second. You want it all . . . and that's okay, as long as it is all lined up in order together.

**KEY THINGS TO CONSIDER**

Other than coming across as arrogant (remember, demeanor is key), there are other errors that can be easy to be aware of when negotiating:

1. Really consider the offer. Some may hear an initial salary offer, deem it too low, and turn down the offer. You may indeed end up not accepting the position, but only do so after negotiating without success.

2. It isn't the company's fault you need more money. When you negotiate, you never want to say, "Well, I have enormous student loans to pay back"; "I subsidized my

college living expenses with a Visa and now have a rather large bill"; or "I was really sick sophomore year and have a huge medical bill I'm paying off."

It isn't the company's problem you have bills, but it *is* to the company's advantage to hire someone who can offer skills and contribute to the growth of the organization. When you negotiate, talk only about what you can bring to the table, not what you need to take from it.

3. Don't demand to be paid as much as "a friend who does the same job and makes this amount." Work out your own salary. This isn't to say you shouldn't know what other people make; you should definitely know comparable salaries for comparable jobs. Do your research. Great websites to visit are PayScale (*www.payscale.com*) and Salary.com (*www.salary.com*) to learn what the going range is for any field.

4. Pick a salary range, not a number. It will do you no good to have a fixed number in your head. Figure out a range you want to make. Remember, make sure the range you envision is congruent with what is appropriate for the type of field/position/career you are seeking.

   If you would love to make $32k, have the idea of $30k to $35k as an acceptable range. But this is for your information only. If you reveal this is your range, you will negate the opportunity to also try to negotiate additional perks in your compensation package. Remember, don't get stuck on a particular number, instead, be open to different options.

5. Consider the whole package. Sometimes a company has a monetary budget and it is what it is. If the company can't offer more money, seek additional forms of compensa-

tion that work to your benefit. Be creative. Go ahead and try to negotiate more vacation time, immediate medical benefits (many companies have a two to three-month waiting period), stock options, bonuses, or telecommuting options.

6. Don't give out past salary info. If you already have a salary history, don't give this information out. If asked, you can respond a few different ways:

- "First, I'd like to hear the range for this position."
- "I'm open to negotiation and want to hear all the pieces of the compensation package (vacation, company perks, health care)."

Sometimes there is just no escaping having to give this information—some employers will specifically ask for a salary history and will not take no for an answer (in fact, not giving it could disqualify you as a candidate). You have to give it. But you can also add this tag line (this is where your research pays off), "After doing some research, I know this type of position pays in this xyz range." They'll be impressed and know you expect to meet these requirements.

7. Pick your battles. If you really do want the position and want to work for the company but the compensation package needs a little boosting, just pick the pieces of greatest importance to you. You can't negotiate it all (money, benefits, vacation). Decide what you want and only negotiate those points. You'll appear truly confident and full of conviction in what you're looking to achieve.

8. It's not personal. Honestly, sometimes the person offering you the job has her hands tied. There just isn't any wiggle room on what you truly want. The company has a budget, and this much was allotted; it is what it is. But it isn't about you. If they didn't like you or didn't want to give you the position and have you join their team, the job would have never been offered.

9. Know what you can contribute. When you negotiate for the things just mentioned, you want to reinforce the deserving factor by confirming all you can contribute to the company. List your strengths with confidence, because they already know them or they wouldn't have offered you the position. Just be sure to be realistic about what you can offer and what to expect in return.

## ADVICE FROM THE CORNER OFFICE
**Michelle Poxson, an HR executive, gives these tips:**

- Have the company explain how they arrived at the current offer. Once they walk you through it, you may be surprised to understand it makes sense. Good companies don't "low ball" prospective talent and really consider everything.

- If you still are not satisfied, think *compromise* and focus on your most important "hot button."

- If the salary number is not where you want it to be, ask if the employer would consider reviewing you for an early merit increase if you show results based on agreed upon goals at six months.

## GET IT IN WRITING

After an agreement is made, ask for the offer in writing. Once you get the letter, be sure it includes each point agreed upon. Don't be shy about asking for this confirmation. In fact, most companies automatically send it, because it protects them as much as it does you. ■

### cheat sheet

Do know it is acceptable to negotiate salary or additional benefits.

Don't have a sense of entitlement when negotiating.

Do be confident—not shy—and make requests to benefit yourself.

Don't take anything personally.

Don't have a fixed number in your head— know the range you're willing to take.

Do get everything in writing before accepting an offer.

Don't try to negotiate every point; do pick your "hot button."

## CHAPTER 15

# Fend Off the Faux Pas

## WORKPLACE ETIQUETTE

> "It takes twenty years to build a reputation and five minutes to ruin it. If you think about that, you'll do things differently."
>
> WARREN BUFFET

So you've scored the job. Congratulations! Surely you want to make a positive impression on your boss and coworkers as you make your way to the career you want.

You might think etiquette is a dated concept confined to old TV shows and out-of-print Emily Post books, but manners are not only timeless, they are powerful tools by which you impress others. Plus, don't forget, your supervisors and managers are of a generation who may still even own a copy of an Emily Post book!

People take notice if someone is decent and polite. And even more than this, they notice if you are inappropriate or ill mannered. Nothing leaves a more negative impression than the proverbial faux pas.

There are specific behaviors considered sizeable don'ts in the business world that you'll want to avoid at all costs. Not only will these actions rob you of your integrity, but they may cost you your hard-earned job or a place on a committee you'd love to serve on. Let's take a look at a few of the most obnoxious:

## GOSSIP

No matter how juicy you think the details of your coworker's affair with the parking attendant may be, unless you work for TMZ or the *National Enquirer*, it's not your job to report the story to others. Gossip is a deadly bug that spreads with brutal force, and it will eventually come back to bite you. Even private, off-site conversations can make it back to the office. If you have to vent, vent to friends who have no idea who the heck you're talking about! You don't want your fellow employees to classify you as a notorious gossip, so take to heart something your parents have told you a thousand times: "If you can't find something nice to say, don't say anything at all."

**ADVICE FROM THE CORNER OFFICE**
Joanne Coghill, assistant vice president human resources for a large mortgage bank, says: "It is not professional to gossip, surf the web, etc. in the workplace. Keep a professional attitude. Don't forward nonwork-related (chain) e-mails. What you e-mail at work can be discovered since the e-mail and computer are company property."

Similar to gossip, badmouthing your boss or coworkers is an unacceptable act in the workplace or on your personal time. Instead, to be successful, develop patterns of speech that lift others up not knock them down. Remember, you won't make yourself seem any more capable by talking others down; you only advance by the measure of your own skills. To make someone look bad in the eyes of others is unkind and unethical.

The best decision to make when you have an issue to resolve is to be the bigger person and take a reasonable and proper course of action to fix the problem. Spite and tattling won't produce anything but a bad reputation.

## CHATTY CATHY

Babbling is another office don't. When you hit it off with those around you, you can get started and sometimes find it hard to stop. But even if you can multitask effectively (work and converse simultaneously), it can be disruptive to those around you and can hinder others' ability to do their job. Often, people are too polite to tell you to be quiet, so you want be sensitive to the needs of those around you. (This includes phone conversations as well.)

## CLIQUES

Making friends at work can be a wonderful advantage to working in a busy office. When coworkers hit it off, the actual work can be so much more pleasant because there's a social element involved. But when job peers hit it off too well, sometimes the "in group" forms into an exclusive clique, alienating others. This is not to say you must hang out with everyone you work with. You may actually make a few good friends and have nothing in common with the rest, which is perfectly understandable. But this should not keep you from being inclusive and approachable to everyone at the office. You definitely don't want your attitude to imply, "You're not as enjoyable as my selected friends and therefore not worthy of my time or attention." Plus, you never know when you'll be tapped to work closely on a project with someone who hasn't been included.

## LUNCH

Contrary to a clique-prone environment, an unsociable office can be a difficult place to work. A little bit of mingling can go a long way to helping you define yourself as a competent and well-rounded person.

If you are invited to lunch by your colleagues and have to decline because you have too much work, fair enough. But if you decline every time you are asked to join the group, you may be presumed to be stuck up. Socializing with fellow employees helps build a team spirit and can make your work even more enjoyable.

If you tend to be shy, here's a little social secret: people love to talk about themselves, so ask them questions that are likely to generate a long-winded answer. Questions such as "What attracted you to this field?" or "How do you juggle your work and mothering responsibilities?" will help you break the ice.

## FOR THE LOVE OF THE WEB

Most companies will give you access to the Internet. These days most companies and employees can't function without it. Someone is always researching something. But when the surfing gets out of control, you may be risking your job. Many companies have filters to block inappropriate sites from being surfed. Even checking your MySpace profile, the ESPN site, Internet shopping, or e-mailing your new love interest are unacceptable behaviors on company time. You definitely don't want to be part of IM chats either—with friends or coworkers—that are of a social nature.

**ADVICE FROM THE CORNER OFFICE**
**Michelle Poxson, an HR executive, says:**

- Showing maturity is really important for college students, especially when being young can bring unfair stereotypes. Employers already know they need to train you with additional skills. What they want is potential and professionalism.
- There is a lot more research, training, and focus on how employee behaviors and teamwork can impact the productivity of a business. Many companies will go after this in the interview and have integrated this into their performance review process, too.

The computer you have been assigned to belongs to your employer, and unless your boss has specifically granted you these special privileges, save your personal computer activity for your personal computer. Stick to the professional research at hand.

Also, even if you see others surfing the web, err on the side of caution. Why take the chance?

## E-MAIL ETIQUETTE

We've all done it: sent an e-mail off in a hurry. A note meant to relay mild dismay is interpreted as forceful and mean. A message full of our witty humor comes across as a too-sarcastic, not-so-funny blunder. In the working world, e-mail etiquette is crucial, and careful consideration should be given to how the message will be perceived. There's no nonverbal or inflection of vocal tone to reinforce the mood of the message. When you talk with someone, you can see anger or humor in his or her eyes. You can watch someone shrug her shoulders, use her hands, or raise her eyebrows. Those nonverbal messages often confirm (or contradict) what is being said for true meaning and understanding of the words.

To make sure your messages are perceived as you meant them, here are a few helpful hints gathered after asking savvy HR professionals, research, and our own experiences:

- If an e-mail makes you angry, wait at least twenty-four hours before sending a reply. The cooling-off period is necessary to diffuse your own emotions, making you better able to communicate your thoughts.
- Unless the recipient is completely familiar with your humor, avoid sarcasm, which is easily misinterpreted.
- AVOID TYPING IN ALL UPPERCASE. IT COMES ACROSS AS A DIRECT ORDER AND/OR ANGER THAT TURNS PEOPLE OFF.
- When replying, truly determine if it's necessary to reply to all. A list was recently released about workplace etiquette annoyances, and the top complaint was replying to the sender by hitting, "Reply to all." For example, if you are asked to attend a presentation, the group doesn't

need to take the time to read that you can't attend because you have a dentist appointment. Unless you're asked to reply this way—don't!"

- Double-check the "To" field. Are you sending the e-mail to the right person? The last thing you want to do is send a confidential e-mail to someone who isn't privy to the information.

- Be sure to intermix personal contact and phone conversations with e-mail correspondence. E-mail shouldn't be a substitute for relationship building. People should still see your "live" personality.

- Reread the e-mail. Does it say you'll attach something? Did you remember to attach it? Are there grammatical or spelling errors?

- Messages shouldn't be forward without permission. When you receive a message, it was meant for you. It should be regarded as the same as if the person came to your office or picked up the phone; it was a private conversation.

- When composing (and sending) an e-mail, ask yourself, "Would I say this to the person's face?" It's easy to use e-mail as a way to avoid a face-to-face conversation, but the message can still be analyzed as to whether it is appropriate to say these words to someone.

- Wording is everything: "I can't believe you gave me this project when you know how busy I am. I'm so frustrated I could just quit" could easily be written as, "This project came at a time when my workload was excessive and I'm worried that I won't be able to give it my all."

- When sending e-mail, make the subject line specific. It really helps to alert the receivers what the message is in regards to, and it also makes it easier to find for future reference.

- When replying to a question, it is best to copy the question into the reply portion of your e-mail and then provide your response. When someone gets a message that simply reads "Yes," it appears to be curt and can also baffle the reader if he or she forgot what was asked. On the other hand, e-mail is meant to be brief, so spare your readers any insignificant details. Be sure to include your name and all of your contact information at the bottom so your recipient doesn't have to take the time to fish for it.

E-mail is a great tool, but it's just that: a tool. When you put thought into messages, it enhances and grows your relationships.

## THE PHONE IS RINGING

Returning phone calls is vital in the professional world. It is amazing how many people don't follow up on messages left or requests requested. Even if you don't yet have an answer to the caller's question, call back to explain you're working on getting the information. It makes a huge difference! And if there is someone else who can help resolve the issue, pass this info along to that person as well.

When your phone rings, many employers ask you to identify yourself and your department when answering. Easy enough! However, the key to phone etiquette is to answer without sounding annoyed even though you're desperately trying to meet a deadline. Remember, the other person doesn't know why you're frazzled. But if this is the case, let the person know and politely ask what he needs and ask for a time and/or date to respond to the request. You also want your outgoing message to be personable and professional. And make sure your voicemail system is working properly and purged routinely so it doesn't tell the caller that the mailbox is full or ring indefinitely.

Personal calls happen. You're at the office for at least eight hours, you have a life, and sometimes things need to be taken care of. Employers understand this. In fact, you may hear your boss call about her electric bill, too. It's the personal, chatty calls that are troublesome for employers (and for those who sit around you in other cubicles if you're in this type of environment). Of course, the best type of call is the call on your own time—take a break and use your cell phone in the breakroom, outside, or in your car. Texting should also be done with discretion.

## INTERRUPTIONS

Disrupting a meeting can sometimes be inevitable. Perhaps your boss is the middle of a presentation yet awaiting an important call that she has asked you to be on the listen for. When letting her know, be considerate of the others in the group and acknowledge that you are aware of the fact that you're interrupting their valuable time. Just be sure the reason you are making an interruption is legitimate. A matter might seem urgent but in reality can wait until the end of an important meeting to be resolved.

## AN ETHICAL TIME

Every company usually has a code of ethics, and you'll probably receive a copy during your initiation period. Violating any part of this code can have grave consequences. If you have questions or need clarification about anything, you definitely want to ask right away. Keep in mind that being let go on an ethical violation (even unknowingly) will likely blow your chances of getting a reference from your boss when you apply for your next job. Know your company's code so you can protect yourself against any unknowing violations.

If it's against company policy for you to receive gifts from clients, then you'll have to politely refuse the offering. Yes, that iPod looks pretty darn appealing, but it's not worth taking it if it jeopardizes your job. And just because certain behaviors may not be on the list does not mean you have carte blanche. For example, be considerate of your coworkers, be courteous to clients, and don't take home office supplies!

## THE CLOCK IS TICKING

The time you are asked to show up to work is not a suggestion. To give or take five or ten minutes is not a good idea, unless you want your boss to note that you have an issue with being on time. And when a meeting is called at 2:00 P.M. that doesn't mean show up at 2:04, or the memo would have indicated 2:04 as the start time. One of the most worthwhile habits you can develop professionally is to be prompt and punctual. Show up to work on time, and show up to your appointments at the time you were asked to attend. Don't be inconsiderate of others and make them wait for you, especially if you are chronically late.

## A LITTLE LOVE

Working in close proximity with people, there may be the temptation to take business relationships to romantic ones. Even if the company doesn't have a policy against interoffice dating, it is not advisable. It can turn a perfectly good job into something awkward and uncomfortable. And, unfortunately, if the relationships tanks, the awkwardness could be magnified by twenty.

Flirting can be fun, especially if your cubicle mate is good-looking, but your coworkers will probably not find your behavior as enjoyable as you do, and it will likely annoy the boss (something you never want to do). Flirting can disrupt a woman's professional credibility much more quickly than it can a man's. There's an age-old stereotype that if a girl is not as qualified as she needs to be, she can get what she wants if she can flirt her way there. It sounds discriminatory and narrow-minded, but don't fall into this trap, even if you're not aware you're doing so. You really want your coworkers to take you seriously. It is hard to for them to do this if they see you as someone to hook up with.

Even innocent flirting could be misconstrued as inappropriate. No doubt there are a host of couples who met at work and have found true and lasting love, but if you're intent on dating those with whom you work, keep your romantic behaviors beyond the borders of the office environment. While at work, conduct yourself professionally. You're being paid to do a job, not to troll for whom you'll be wining and dining this Saturday night.

## OFFICE POLITICS

The boss's buddy gets the best leads. The hot, long-legged secretary's tardiness is overlooked. Welcome to the world of injustice. Working with other people will open your eyes to a host of inequities such as favoritism, biases, and other unpleasantries. But while most of these practices are unfair, they are usually not illegal.

If you find yourself in a situation that does warrant legal action (such as if you are a victim of harassment or discrimination), consult a business attorney to evaluate your issue. Otherwise, you can spin yourself into a tizzy trying to right every wrong. Just remember this: maintain your own integrity and don't reduce yourself to any questionable ethical behavior. You are only responsible for your own actions. You can hope that unrighteousness will be caught and corrected in the workplace, but if it isn't, just make sure you are singled out because you've done the right thing.

## CORPORATE CULTURE

Every company has a culture. Even no culture is a culture. The company's culture is the tone that employees learn to live within. Some companies are formal and conservative while others are casual and laid back. Some are lots of fun; others are conservative. Before taking a job, ask questions, do research, and look around at other employees to ascertain if a culture is right for you.

Part of your company's culture can be as simple as whether eating at your desk is acceptable. If you work at an establishment where the ambiance is more carefree, you may be permitted to eat at your desk. If so, munch away! But before you dig into your lunch, be certain your space is food approved. And you may want to reconsider a tuna sandwich—or anything else aromatic. It might taste great, but your coworkers may not enjoy that lingering fish stench all afternoon.

If your office environment is formal or conservative, you will probably have more rules by which to abide. Be sure you're advised of what those are and hold to them. If you want to keep your job, keep to the rules!

For every etiquette dilemma there is an appropriate solution, especially when it comes to what not to do in business. Check out Lydia Ramsey's website at *www.mannersthatsell.com*, where a comprehensive list of how to mind your manners at work can be found. And definitely make a friend in the HR department—don't be afraid to ask questions, that is why they're there!

Keep in mind you are a reflection of the department for which you work and, more importantly, the company. Employers know right off the bat which employees can be trusted to fulfill expectations and who can't be relied upon. Whether you are aware of it or not, you are constantly being sized up, not just on your work performance, but by how you get along with your coworkers, how polite and ethical you are, and how loyal you are to the company. Being aware of this and working to always come out on top will help you quickly propel your career forward.

## DEFENSE BELONGS ON THE FOOTBALL FIELD

In the right context, being on the defensive makes sense; however, there's no need for defensiveness at the workplace. The greatest gift anyone can give you is constructive feedback.

Constructive criticism isn't always easy to hear, and the person giving it doesn't always articulate it in the proper way. But once you get past all of that, hearing what you can improve on is the surest way to continue to plow forward to success. If you approach the feedback with vigor, you're the one who will win as you change your tactics and learn from your mistakes (or your not knowing). So thank someone for feedback—he or she really is doing you a favor, even if at the time it doesn't seem so.

Also, avoid being on the defensive when someone asks you to do something you may not want to do or something you think

## cheat sheet

**Don't badmouth your boss or coworkers.**

**Don't gossip.**

**Do stay away from participation in restrictive cliques.**

**Don't make personal phone calls.**

**Don't spend time surfing the web when you should be working.**

**Don't be the office flirt.**

**Do be politically correct.**

**Do be on time to meetings or appointments.**

**Don't be defensive at work.**

**Don't get caught up in or instigate inappropriate humor or jokes at the workplace.**

is beneath you. Your superior will respect your willingness and you'll be rewarded in the long run. Remember, if you someday become a manager, or even start your own business, you'll need to know the basics and the business from the ground up.

### EFFECTIVE USE OF HUMOR

Everyone loves a good laugh; it helps you build camaraderie. But appropriate humor is key. Let the laughter stem from the fun and rapport you build with colleagues over everyday light-heartedness. Avoid falling into giddy humor, which *Webster's Dictionary* defines as "frivolous." You don't need to tell bawdy jokes to be liked. In fact, there is no need to stand for, listen to, or participate in the barroom humor in the workplace. If you keep your pride and respect, you won't get sucked into the conversations.

Also, do not take part in inappropriate jesting. Even with the sexual harassment training you'll most likely receive, some workplaces still offer a relaxed environment. But that doesn't mean it is ok to tell the joke you heard last Saturday night. If you wouldn't tell a joke to your boss, don't tell it at all.

Humor in the workplace is a fine line. Build a rapport with coworkers by having fun with professional humor. ∎

## CHAPTER 16

# Find a Balance

## NICE VERSUS NOT

"What separates the winners from the losers is how a person reacts to each new twist of fate."

DONALD TRUMP

In college, people get typecast rather fast. Almost from the beginning of a school year there are certain peers who are considered friendly while others are thought to be cold. Some are social; others are bookworms. In professional circles, personalities are rated as well, often erroneously. For example, have you ever noticed that women who are firm are often described as bitchy? And why are self-assured men often described as jerks? Is it because they are, or because some people, in an effort to retain their seemingly endangered position of power, believe they have to be aggressive to be effective? To be perceived as competent, young professionals must find a comfortable balance between rigidity and softness.

## A BALANCING ACT

Those who are firm can be deemed dependable and consistent. Those who are soft can be deemed kind, but can also be thought of as pushovers. Are these mutually exclusive traits, or can there be a happy balance? While there is never an excuse for rudeness, impoliteness, or inappropriate behavior in a work environment, softness does not mean that you have to change your conviction or course of action simply because you are being challenged. Stand by your beliefs. There is a fine line, but it's a clearly defined one that serves as the tight rope on which an authoritative and confident person must walk.

A strong person must be clever, discriminating, sharp, and respectful to be taken seriously in the working world. Remember, you never want to be seen as overly aggressive, which can be difficult when saying no in the office. Learning to reformulate and soften words to respectfully deliver a less than desirable message is the most significant way that a young professional can retain his or her authority.

Oftentimes, gender stereotypes translate from societal norms into the corporate office. Men are often raised to perform and achieve, starting from participation in Little League. While lessons about teamwork and achievement learned on the field can be advantageous in a professional environment, men can also learn to be ruthlessly competitive. This aptitude can drive them to push full speed ahead, sometimes at the expense of others and their feelings.

Women, on the other hand, have stereotypically been raised to be helpers and givers. Yes, women have made great strides in business and culture, but they are generally thought of as more nurturing than their male counterparts. This characteristic can serve women well, but it can also be a giant hurdle in their ability to say no to others.

There will be times, for both men and women, when you'll need to say use the dreaded word no, especially when your social (home) life interferes with your work. But at work you'll be met with opportunities to take on more responsibility, so it's best to learn how to effectively decline and still be considered capable yet kind.

**ADVICE FROM THE CORNER OFFICE**

La'Trise Smith, assistant vice president of human resources at Huntington Bank, says: "I believe in having balance in all that you do. Stick with your polices and guidelines, but have a humane approach. If you stick with this you can feel confident and let your yeses be 'Yes' and your nos be 'No.' This doesn't mean that you are going to please all the people all of the time, but typically they will go away with a better understanding of the whys behind it. Be fair and consistent in your employment practices and you can't go wrong."

## THE ART OF SAYING "NO"

Today, most employees protest about having too much on their plate. With corporate cutbacks and a streamlined staff, a normal workload can often be overwhelming. However, cutting out specific tasks can be daunting, simply because you'd either have to decline a request for help, or you'd have to relinquish a particular area of responsibility to someone else.

You can't say no all the time, even if you think a task is beneath you, outside of your job description, or if you just don't want to do it. By doing this, you'll just earn a bad reputation. But there will be times you just have to say "no" so your other projects don't suffer.

Choose your "nos" sparingly and wisely, but don't be afraid to graciously decline if you have an honest concern; however, do so carefully. You don't want to appear lazy or unwilling to lend a hand, and often the guilt you experience by denying a plea for help is more agonizing than performing the actual task. However, saying "no" doesn't have to be intimidating; it is often liberating and empowering, and if you take everything that is given to you, your lack of resistance may make you resentful and will negatively affect your performance anyway. In addition, your other priorities will suffer simply because you have become spread too thin, and juggling priorities becomes a greater burden.

Before you master the art of the "no," you must learn to set personal boundaries and preserve your sense of self-respect. Value your time and your physical and mental health enough to learn when something, even if it is a noble chore, will infringe upon your overall well-being. You rob yourself (and your family) of precious resources when you become overextended.

You don't want to start a new job distributing a string of noes. But if you are asked to serve on a variety of committees, participate in gift exchanges out of your budget range, or are asked to engage in social invites you think will distract you from your goals, then you can certainly bow out. It is not a good idea to decline an assignment handed down from your boss just because you think you have enough work on your desk and need to be out by 5:00 P.M. sharp, and you don't want to decline too many offers or projects, lest you be seen as unsocial or unproductive. You also don't have to accept everything thrown your way; the key is finding the right balance.

Declining with grace, however, is a learned art as you can come off as abrasive or rude if you respond without forethought. When you must turn down a task, it's important to say "no" with a persuasive voice. Instead of saying, "I'm not sure I'll be able to get to it," try "My time is already devoted to other commitments and I just don't have the time necessary to do this project justice." Lay aside meekness and acquiescence; choose to be convincing and unwavering. If challenged or made to feel guilty, you can disagree without being disagreeable; simply say, "I would like to help you, but I know what is realistic to do a good job or stick to what is realistic for my time schedule."

Some prefer the stalling technique: "Let me think about it and I'll get back to you." This can sometimes be effective, because when you come back with a no, it shows you have taken the time to thoughtfully consider whether your participation is realistic. This lends your refusal more credibility. However, don't use it every time. It can also backfire, because it demonstrates you don't have the wherewithal to affirmatively state at the given time that you're not able to do the project. In fact, your stalling may unintentionally harm the project's timeline. So, as with everything, be honest and use in moderation.

What if you need to approach your superior because you've been asked to do something outside of a realistic timeframe with other projects on your plate? Try approaching your boss with one of the following three techniques:

1. Offer a solution-based alternative. Determine what works best to get the task done and offer it as an alternative. For example, instead of staying late to complete a job, offer to take it home and work on it over the weekend.
2. Request a private meeting with your boss and express your desire to perform well, but explain your time limitations are being overextended. Propose a discussion as to how to make it more realistic.

3. Ask for help. Simply state (confidently) that you need additional time and/or assistance and/or knowledge to complete the task on time. Be honest about discussing you don't want to do a mediocre job. This is a tricky slope, but speak confidently so it doesn't appear as if you can't handle the project but rather as though you're professional enough to assess what is needed for the project to be superior.

There may be times when you're asked to perform a task defying your moral or spiritual convictions. Stating, "No, I'm not comfortable with this," will reveal your sense of honor and passion while enabling you to decline the plea. But feel free to offer options or different solutions that you would feel comfortable pursuing. Saying no actually becomes easier with practice; once you learn that you can honor your boundaries and preserve your sanity by not taking on one more thing, you will gain more confidence when judging your limitations in the future. Plus, you'll learn that people will still like and respect you even when you do say "no"!

## DON'T BE ANGRY

Remember, even when you have to turn down a proposal, do so with a lot of grace. Show off your people skills! Shouting, swearing, or becoming impatient are only signs of poor communication skills as well as a total lack of self-control. Once you're tagged as an "exploder," you can be certain most people will avoid you altogether. Anyone constantly grumbling or yelling about the workload is usually regarded as a liability or a lawsuit waiting to happen.

It's important to stay calm and focused whenever you have to reject a proposition or take a firm stand. Remember, being resolved and assertive is good, but being angry is bad.

Anger leads to all sorts of problems, both physical and psychological. Whether you are screaming or just seething internally, you may experience increased blood pressure, increased heart rate, and gnawing guilt; anger is not good for you. Studies reveal younger workers display more anger than older ones because people in time learn to master or control their emotions. While everyone experiences anger, it's the ones who can put that aside and express their feelings with restraint and strength of mind who will be heard.

A little trick: When you want to explode or yell at someone, don't talk to that person until the next day. You'll have calmed down, slept on it, and be able to articulate your concerns much more professionally and maturely. It works every time. You can even go home and write the person a faux letter; you should never send it, but it will allow you to release your pent-up emotion over the situation.

Some anger is healthy. If you are the target of injustice or prejudice, it's important to express how you feel, just do so in the right way. Follow company protocol and talk to the right people; your employer is legally required to prevent a hostile workplace. (So if you're the obstinate one, you'll probably hear about it, too!) In 2006, 441 people were killed and 15,000 injured in physical attacks at work, according to the Bureau of Labor Statistics. So if you're the one with the angry side, your employer doesn't know whether it is an innocent flare-up or a violent or brutal outcry, so you bet they'll take notice.

If you just can't relieve your anger, go work out, write in a journal, talk to a trusted friend, or consult with the company's in-house EAP (employee assistance program) counselor. You should certainly get to a rational point before you start unleashing your fury. Yelling is never productive; it just makes you look like an idiot. And if your anger is completely out of control, consider enlisting in an anger management program. Learning to be in control of your temper will serve you well, even beyond the office setting.

## SEXUAL HARASSMENT

Most companies have a solid antiharassment policy. Be sure to read it and ask someone in the human resources department to clarify if you don't understand the details.

You should never allow yourself to be the victim or instigator of sexual harassment, as this is an unacceptable and punishable offense. Sexual harassment is a form of sex discrimination that violates Title VII of the Civil Rights Act of 1964. According to the U.S. Equal Employment Opportunity Commission, sexual harassment is defined as "Unwelcome sexual advances, requests for sexual favors, and other verbal or physical conduct of a sexual nature constitutes sexual harassment when submission to or rejection of this conduct explicitly or implicitly affects an individual's employment, unreasonably interferes with an individual's work performance or creates an intimidating, hostile or offensive work environment."

The EEOC (Equal Employment Opportunity Commission) also notes sexual harassment can occur in a variety of circumstances, including but not limited to the following:

- The victim as well as the harasser may be a woman or a man. The victim does not have to be of the opposite sex.

- The harasser can be the victim's supervisor, an agent of the employer, a supervisor in another area, a coworker, or a nonemployee.
- The victim does not have to be the person harassed, but could be anyone affected by the offensive conduct.
- Unlawful sexual harassment may occur without economic injury to or discharge of the victim.
- The harasser's conduct must be unwelcome.

If you think you are a victim of harassment by a coworker or superior, be sure to take proper action by reporting it to a top-level superior. Don't think you'll avoid making waves by keeping silent. Besides, there are antiretaliation laws (meaning you are protected from any retaliation by the company or supervisors for speaking up). And you actually may do your reputation (and legal woes) more harm than good by not reporting information. If conditions don't improve, seek legal advice.

**ADVICE FROM THE CORNER OFFICE**
La'Trise Smith, assistant vice president of human resources at Huntington Bank, advises employees to "Understand what's going on in your camp. Don't turn a blind eye to inappropriate behavior even if it seems like it's no big deal to you. Don't be a victim to that old saying, 'What's done in the dark will come out in the light.' I wouldn't want to be the one holding the bag when the lights are turned on. Handle it quickly with the appropriate action."

## cheat sheet

Do learn to reformulate words to respectfully decline work.

Do use your noes sparingly and wisely.

Don't be afraid to graciously decline if you have an honest concern.

Do offer a solution-based alternative if you are unable to complete any given task for whatever reason.

Don't allow anger to be part of your speech.

Don't participate in anything that even hints at sexual harassment.

Be aware that the most innocent and seemingly harmless joke can cause trouble. The anguish and embarrassment you'll face is not worth the fun you might be having when telling it.

Whether you're dealing with severe offenses, normal annoyances, or battling how to behave in order to be taken seriously at work, remember you are being watched by your fellow employees, as well as your supervisors. Conduct yourself with professionalism, be assertive and self-composed, and don't lose your cool and you'll be fine. Always remember, your career depends as much on your behavior as it does on your performance. ■

## CHAPTER 17

# Go to the Head of the Class

## LEADERSHIP SKILLS FOR THE LONG RUN

> "The key to successful leadership today is influence, not authority."
>
> KEN BLANCHARD

There are many different people, leaders, books, seminars, and websites that all have different views of leadership qualities. The bottom line is whether or not people want to not have to—follow a leader.

Notice the previous sentence didn't say "good" leader. There have been some barbaric leaders out there and people want to follow them, but it doesn't make them *good*. Nonetheless, they are leaders.

So if you want to be a good (or even great!) leader, you also want to have an ethical and integrity-filled value system guiding your principles. Leading involves heading up a project, team, or company and finding success. Whether it is a profit-making marketing idea, an administrative system overhaul, a development of a new idea for a product, or an IT department that can answer and fix technology problems, leadership is taking the lead.

Following are some universal ideas that equate to "good" leadership qualities.

## A GENUINE INTEREST IN PEOPLE

To be a good leader you have to want to genuinely see people succeed. Most people who are in successful positions have had help along the way. Yes, they absolutely have the knowledge, skills, tenacity, and the drive to get them to where they want to be, but they've also had some help. And the help comes from others who genuinely wanted to see them succeed.

**ADVICE FROM THE CORNER OFFICE**
**Michelle Poxson, an HR executive, says:**

- Great leaders build trust before they start managing. People need to know you care and are working in their best interest. Once this is established, you can discuss performance issues or roadblocks without others taking it personally.
- Great leaders are coaches. They ask more then tell. They let others struggle a little to learn but are ready with simple, practical advice if needed.
- Great leaders are versatile. They consider and adapt quickly to everyone else's style, not the other way around. This allows them to get to the task quicker.
- Great leaders manage their talent. They recognize stars, develop the middle, and ensure that consistently poor performers are managed out.

If you take a genuine interest in people, they will take a genuine interest in you. Study after study shows that people don't leave companies, they leave people. Not liking managers is usually the gripe employees give when leaving a position—even more so than salary! This speaks volumes about leadership and about the type of manager people want to work for. An easy way to show interest is to give credit where credit is due. If someone else deserves credit or to share in the credit, being vocal about acknowledging other peoples' work goes a long way!

Something else that is really important: empower others, don't micromanage. Have faith in those on your team—give them the tools (training and support) to either succeed or fail. Once they have learned enough to do things on their own, let them! When they succeed, give them credit. When they fail, determine the extent of the damage and teach, train, lead, and develop their skills so they don't fail again.

Always give people the benefit of the doubt. They said something that was misinterpreted? Let them explain. They did something not on par with company behavioral standards? Let them explain. They made a mistake? Let them explain their thought process and reasoning. Yes, there will be those who take advantage, and they can be dealt with on an individual basis. But give people the benefit of the doubt. Doing so demonstrates you really want to see them succeed!

## RELATE TO OTHERS

For a long time, empathy, sympathy, and understanding got a bad rap. They were seen as signs of weakness. Now book after book is written about how necessary they are within the workplace. This doesn't mean you should be a pushover, but having the ability to relate and understand the people you work with creates a bond that translates into respect within the workplace.

This, of course, assumes you've surrounded yourself with a good team. You always want to hire and retain the best of the best and treat them as such; relate to them and the respect they have for you will go through the roof.

**ADVICE FROM THE CORNER OFFICE**
**Nichole Addario DiModica, former vice president of operations and human resources for Dualstar Entertainment Group, says being a good leader means:**

- **Being a great communicator and knowing that communication occurs in the speaking *and* the listening.**
- **Surrounding yourself with people who are smart (possibly smarter than you are in a particular area of expertise).**
- **Showing respect. Don't be so wrapped up in getting it. Treat your team members as colleagues and equals. It inspires people to think far past what their current role may be.**
- **Delegating. A great leader knows the "if no one can do it right, I'll just do it myself" attitude does not inspire.**

## KNOW YOUR STUFF

Talent is not enough. Personality is not enough. You have to know what you are talking about. Be good at what you do. Lead in an area where you exceed. Continue to learn and grow and

# CLASS NOTES

## Christine, 26

Christine graduated from Chapman University with a sociology degree and was hired at a large life insurance company as a trainee thanks to **a lead from her mom**. "Most people don't major in insurance, so they get into the business on someone else's recommendation," she says. "I'm glad I did because it's turned out to be really lucrative for me."

Then a **recruiter called her with an opportunity** to try her hand as an insurance broker for a smaller company, and she interviewed for the position and got the job. But she soon realized that the underwriting side of the insurance business is where she is most gifted, so she transferred into this department. Four years into her young career, Christine is now the senior underwriter at the company, a position requiring travel about 50 percent of the month. She believes her confidence, communication skills, and leadership abilities were key factors in her ability to get the positions for which she's applied. "I always felt competent and believed I could get the job and I think this always came across," she says.

Christine believes employers today are looking for **self-starters, go-getters, and team players** who work with others but can also function autonomously. When she hires employees, she looks for candidates who are poised, polished, have good communication skills, and are willing to give it their all.

stay apprised of new technology, new developments, and new ways of looking at things.

## COMMUNICATE WELL

Communication is a must for great leaders. If you know your skills but can't communicate, you can't lead other people to achieve goals. Communication moves a company forward. One-on-one meetings, company seminars, newsletters . . . these are all ways of communicating the company culture and vision. If this is something you aren't comfortable with, you really need to take steps to improve—even excel—in this area.

## BE HONEST

You need to possess superior skills, but, at the same time, if you don't know something, be honest and say so.

Be open about the vision of the company. Be honest about what is happening within your industry. Integrity plays a huge part in people trusting you, what you say, and what you stand for. Once someone questions your integrity, it is often too difficult to regain the trust necessary to lead people to success. Remember, actions speak louder than words. Lead by example, and this often starts with just being honest.

## 20/20 VISION

It has been said that managers manage but leaders have vision—a clear vision. Being a leader is not just about telling people what to do, following the rules, and staying on course to reach a goal. It is about having a clear understanding of the bigger picture. Leaders create the path that their employees follow and are able to bypass the current thinking to look at situations in a new, innovative way. This is imperative for success. Leaders constantly use their vision to make things better and more successful, including the careers of their employees.

## A THICK SKIN

Not everyone will like you. Even if you're a great leader, you'll always have some opposition. If you're confident, stick to your vision, and have everyone's best interest at heart, you'll win out in the end.

### ADVICE FROM THE CORNER OFFICE
**Sara Van Wagoner, senior executive, says leaders:**

- Do what they say they're going to do.
- Are respectful of everyone's opinion.
- Are prepared to work hard to get the job done, even if it's not their job.
- Are appreciative of the rest of the team/group.
- Are truthful and show integrity in all they say and do.
- Admit their mistakes, ask for help when needed, and learn from both.
- Laugh and enjoy the work and the people around them—if it's not any fun, then they're in the wrong place.

Don't let those who oppose you discourage you. Instead, know your facts, ideas, and goals and be able to stand up for yourself. Make decisions and stand by them. Take credit for your wins, but if you've made a mistake or a bad decision, take responsibility. This is a fine line but an important one: have humility but also believe in yourself! Don't let opposition get you down.

## GO ABOVE AND BEYOND

Leaders are people who don't know the words, "Not my job." They work hard, strong, and long; they make an effort, sacrifice, and underpromise and overdeliver. Leaders don't stop short of meeting the goals they set and taking the people they lead all the way. They go above and beyond.

## BE LIKEABLE

Above all, good leaders are likeable and approachable! People like being around them and want to follow them *because* they like them. As a leader, examine your own personality and ask yourself if are you likeable. If not, try to figure out why.

If you want to be a leader, then take the reins immediately when you enter a company. This doesn't mean be pushy, bossy, or domineering! Leadership qualities are usually apparent, even if someone is just starting out in an entry-level position. Going into a position showing likeability and a desire to learn, giving and sharing credit, and quickly rising to a position where you can successfully lead a team or complete a project are all signs that demonstrate your leadership skills. People will want to work with you and will trust your ideas and vision.

# CLASS NOTES

Erin, 27

Erin graduated from college with a BA in communication with an emphasis in journalism. Soon after graduation she realized she had a passion for fashion and style and wanted to work within this industry, even though it's a difficult one to break into. She went back to the Fashion Institute of Design and Merchandising and received an associate degree in merchandise marketing **to complement her bachelor's degree**.

Erin's first professional job out of college was as a sales representative (vendor) for a large accessories company where she stayed for a year. Her responsibilities included selling accessories to major department stores and specialty boutiques across the United States and negotiating with vendors on a daily basis. She worked within four different markets where both buyers and sellers, as well as domestic and international consumers, attended the trade shows. Her showroom represented thirteen notable lines of handbags, shoes, beads, and other accessories, and she was also responsible for merchandising the showroom and making lots of cold calls.

Her first position was challenging, but **she went above and beyond** the job description and was able to learn invaluable skills like assertiveness, confidence, and a strong knowledge of the wholesale industry. She had an obvious passion for the fashion industry, which played a huge part in her landing the job and receiving multiple promotions! She later moved out of this industry into a prominent position with another company as an executive recruiter for HR professionals, which she loves. "**My first job really prepared me** for the work I do now, which requires a lot of sales and communication."

## GETTING YOURSELF PROMOTED

Is your goal to grab a promotion? Oftentimes, you have to create your own career paths and/or look to your supervisors and mentors to help you determine the best route. Once you do this, how do you start the upward travel? For starters, when you're in your current position, a good rule to follow is to work like you're already in the job you want, or at least work productively no matter where you are.

Also, when it's time to give credit, be humble. It may seem as though you did all the work on the team project, but it was a team effort nonetheless and should be attributed as so. If you are doing solid work consistently and offering up ideas in think-tank sessions or meetings, superiors will notice. You'll receive the proper credit; someone will be aware.

This being said, it is still important to sell yourself. Take credit for your ideas to some extent. Within context, the squeaky wheel gets the oil. Know your strengths and demonstrate them; talk with your supervisor or mentor about your goals and aspirations. Know how your strengths work to benefit the organization and why you're valuable.

### Apples to Apples: A Case Study

At one company, Michael went in and told the HR manager and owner of the company that he thought he should be promoted to a higher position based on his experience and how much money he'd like to be making.

He then proceeded to say that he couldn't go on working and being committed unless he knew the position (and salary) was out there within a given time frame, and that he knew the promotion was inevitable. Then, and only then, would he would do a good job.

Well, Michael definitely took himself out of the running for any future promotion(s). An employee should excel in his current position, as well as show why he is deserving of every single leadership responsibility that he currently has, or that which is on the future horizon. This is how leadership is demonstrated.

## Useful Strategies

Here are some other tips to help you get ahead:

*Learn new skills:* Be steps ahead in terms of possessing skills critical to the company. Technology is constantly changing— if you change, too, you're invaluable. This includes knowing the latest happenings, news, and developments within your industry. The more you know, the more you *can* know.

*Visit the HR department:* The open positions filter through them. They can also work with you on long-term goals with the company as well as getting the right training and attaining the necessary skill sets. They talk directly with supervisors and can often offer valuable input.

*Make your boss look good:* Having a good working relationship with your supervisor also makes the department look good. And if the department is successful, you'll be successful.

*Have the right venting outlet:* Remember, this person shouldn't be a coworker, no matter how much you may get along. It's awful when someone overhears, or when circumstances change and one of you finds yourself in a supervisory role over the other. Too much insight can be dangerous when roles change and new behaviors are

## cheat sheet

**Don't assume you're a leader just because you have a title.**

**Do constantly improve your knowledge and skills; you have to stay current within your industry.**

**Don't take criticism personally.**

**Don't take credit when it belongs to others.**

**Don't work poorly on a project you didn't want, thinking you'll do better once you get something you're more interested in.**

**Don't sacrifice your integrity, honesty, approachability, or vision for anything.**

expected. Vent to a personal friend or family member; it won't come back to haunt you.

*Go above and beyond:* This isn't to suggest taking on more than you can handle or a project that will keep you at the office an extra two hours every night. But going above and beyond will demonstrate your ability to tackle new projects.

*Ask:* Have a heart-to-heart with your manager, HR, or whoever can help you get to where you want to be. If you find out how to get where you want to be, you get there. In the same way, if there are issues you're not aware of, you can correct the situation, set the story straight, or learn the skills you didn't even know you needed. Asking enables those who can help you to *actually* help you. ∎

## CHAPTER 18

# The Well-Schooled Employee

## CONCLUSION

> "I have missed more than 9,000 shots in my career. I have lost almost 300 games. On twenty-six occasions I have been entrusted to take the game-winning shot . . . and I missed. I have failed over and over and over again in my life. And that is precisely why I succeed."
>
> MICHAEL JORDAN

There's no doubt that as you job search you will face different challenges and hurdles that your parents most likely did not have to confront. Today, an employer almost always expects a college degree. But going beyond expectations is what will help you navigate your career.

These days you have an abundance of advantages when it comes to breaking into the job market. You can utilize social marketing to make connections and present yourself to prospective employers through platforms like Facebook, LinkedIn, Gather, and a multitude of other forums designed to help people connect. Alumni groups now have state-of-the-art websites, which are continually developing social media of their own to benefit their recent graduates.

So now that you have written a solid resume, collected your career search supplies, and made solid contacts, you're ready to hit the job market well equipped and well prepared. And although you should feel proud to have earned your college degree, now you know that it takes more than that impressive diploma to help you on your way to a successful and rewarding profession. Good communication skills and confidence are also of the utmost importance and can guide you onto a path of success. We hope that you will keep this book handy and refer to it when needed. Whether you're just starting to enter the working world or you find yourself making a job switch down the line, you can brush up on your job-search skills by revisiting the information you've just learned.

As you develop your professional skills and experience, you will continually need to update your resume and redesign your cover letter in order to target the specific job you want. Referring to this book will also help you excel in the position you acquire once you start the job, as the information is designed to help you develop into your best professional self.

We hope we have inspired you to reach beyond what you thought was possible to attain your career goals. As a young job seeker, you hold amazing qualities desirable to employers, so use these to your advantage when you venture out into your own personal working world. ■

# Index

# About the Authors

BRIDGET GRAHAM is a human resources manager and consultant for several companies in the Southern California area. She is a former regional human resources manager where she was responsible for five states in the Midwest region, 2,500 employees, ninety store managers, and six district managers. She has hired and trained key individuals, developed and facilitated corporate leadership programs, and has also mediated employee conflict within organizations such Nordstrom Inc., PCR Services Corp. (an environmental consulting company), and Romero Thorsen Design (a top environmental graphic design and branding firm with clients such as Disney and AMC Theatres). She's been in the think tanks with board members and in the trenches with powerful customers and has always held her own. She loves to speak to large groups and has served as a trainer for hundreds of people in corporate orientations and development sessions.

Bridget returned to school in the midst of a successful career to earn a master's degree in communication at Pepperdine University in Malibu, California. A native of Chicago, she moved to West Los Angeles a few years ago and has learned an entirely new culture. She strengthened her ability to meet people, connect, network, and develop relationships.

While pursuing her studies as a full-time student, Bridget began to work for *Malibu Times Magazine* and quickly became the editorial assistant and is now, in addition to consulting in human resources, the part-time assistant editor as well as a freelance writer for both the magazine and its sister newspaper. She is also cofounder and editor of TheSavvyGal.com, a website magazine.

Part of her assistantship at the university was working with undergraduate students in the journalism department. Whether it was writing for the student publications, coaching new writers on style techniques, or editing work, Bridget developed a sense of who those students are and what they are looking to achieve.

A member of Society for Human Resource Professionals, National Communication Association, and the Society of Professional Journalists, Bridget also writes various employee publications such as handbooks, appraisals, and codes of conduct for several companies.

MONIQUE REIDY has a bachelor of arts degree in intercultural communication with a minor in sociology, and a master's degree in communication with an emphasis in journalism from Pepperdine University. Her graduate research focused on the impact of women's magazines on American culture, and she graduated cum laude with both degrees.

A former editor-in-chief for *Westlake Magazine*, Monique currently is the cofounder and art director for TheSavvyGal.com, a web-based magazine. She also writes for a number of other websites, as well as local and international publications.

She has written about travel, fitness, health and beauty, women and business, medicine, parenting, communication and relationships, women's issues, celebrity profiles, and restaurant, film, and book reviews. Prior to pursuing her writing passion, Monique worked as an advertising director, and owned and managed a design firm servicing clients such as the L.A. Dodgers, the USC football team, Showtime Networks, Amgen, Cal Fed Bank, and more.

Monique belongs to the Society of Professional Journalists, the International Association for Relationship Research, the National Communication Association, and the Association for Education in Journalism and Mass Communication.

She is an avid traveler and serves on a number of philanthropic committees. Trilingual, her interests lie in social sciences, fashion, health, and fitness. Monique, a mother of three young adult daughters, lives in Westlake Village, California, with her husband, Dr. Stephen Reidy.